———

It's Getz vs. Reality . . .

What's about 80 times funnier, more offbeat, irreverent and insightful than a Bob Getz column? A whole bookful of Bob Getz!

In this collection of his favorite columns, the popular Wichita Eagle columnist flexes his unique wit to . . .

Write the "definitive" article about love . . . take on the devil and even Oral Roberts . . . reveal shocking stuff women should know about men . . . define real Kansas men and women . . . explore the true meaning of cats, dogs and David Letterman . . . and, among many other things, take a refreshingly tilted look at politics, sports, Sinatra, Michael Jackson, country music, Elvis, Armageddon and James Dean.

A Bookful of

BOB GETZ

By Bob Getz

DEDICATION

To Whit, who gave me a chance;
to Jack, Bob, Tom and Buzz,
who let me loose with columns;
and to Page, Tracy, Chase
and especially Jeannie,
who made me even luckier.

The columns in this book first appeared, in slightly different form,
in The Wichita Eagle.

Printed in the United States of America by Mennonite Press, Inc.,
Newton, Kansas 67114

ISBN 1-880652-11-0
Library of Congress Catalog Number 92-60656

Cover and section front designs by Sara Quinn
Cover photography by Steve Harper
Edited by Chuck Potter

INTRODUCTION

I got my first column on a newspaper when I was 21.

I never got over it.

I tried to.

I figured that one job would be about the extent of my newspaper "career," as I meant to move on to other things.

Three times, I did move on. To lots of other things.

Three times, I returned.

And now, here I am, two decades and some 5,000 columns later, still whacking little keyboard letters, trying frantically to pound them into columns four times a week.

Amazing how fate nudges us around like silly, helpless little chess pieces.

I never meant to go into this business in the first place, never studied for it, never meant to stay in it, and now look what's happened to me.

A book.

Proof for certain that despite my resistance and despite my many happy impulses and detours, I have been lucky enough to have undergone a career as a newspaper columnist.

You can't really beat what I do for a living, in a lot of ways.

I realized that when I was 21, and I feel the same way now.

Actually, I even think that, despite what I may have said in the past, I'd rather be a columnist than be employed as shortstop for the Cleveland Indians. When you're a columnist, you don't have to quit when the legs go.

With the Wichita Eagle, I've labored over about 3,000 columns, give or take a few dozen sweaty deadlines.

Almost all these columns, which cover 16 years with The Eagle, were written under the gun of deadline. Not that they'd be any better if they hadn't been.

Over the years, a lot of readers have asked for a book like this, and I'm delighted it has happened.

Slight changes have been made here and there, most having to do with updating or clarifying parts of columns that time may have rendered a little baffling.

But most "dated" references to former presidents, mayors, my ex-wife, temporarily famous people who have faded into obscurity, etc., have been left alone to avoid a bunch of clumsy notes or changes.

I'd like to thank Glenda Holder Elliott, Deb Kimble, Carolyn Hytche and Barbara Sutton for their help in getting these columns ready, and my handy fiancee, Jeannie Smarsh, for helping with the mammoth task of sorting through thousands of columns to find these.

I also want to thank, especially, the key players behind the book — graphics ace Sara Quinn, nemesis and photo man Steve Harper, publisher Bill Handy, whose idea this was, and, last and most of all, my excellent editor, Chuck Potter. I never fully appreciated these people's talents until I saw them in action.

I owe the most, though, to the man who gave me this special job and forum. I couldn't have asked for a more supportive or ideal boss than Buzz Merritt.

And now maybe I should get out of the way here so you can get on to the proof that I never got over column writing and a career seems to have happened to me.

Wichita, Kan.
May 1992

Table of Contents

Beware of the Reality

Is Earth Going Crazy? How About It, Doc? 2

Just How Good Were the Good Old Days? 4

The Devil and Oral Roberts 6

Waiting for McMahon and $10 Million 9

This Coupon Worth $5 Toward a Nice Divorce 12

Remember When Selling Kiddies Was Illegal? 14

Dear Rex Humbard: PLEASE READ THIS!!! 17

How Long Should Miracles Last? 20

Ain't You Seen Nothin' Yet, Officers? 22

This Is Your Captain Speaking; Shall We Pray? 25

The Most Outrageous Ticket Ever Written? 27

Danny Wants Back in Prison – for Good 30

Proving to Kids There Are No Monsters 32

Contemplating Fame and the Famous

Under the Influence of James Dean 38

Our Kind of Cat, Sinatra Is... 40

Elvis Was Like a Double Overtime 43

Royal Wedding Needed Dwarfs or Mice 45

Roy Orbison – Rock's Least Likely Legend 47

Is Michael Jackson's Success, Well, Weird? 50

Beware of Ozzy – He Bites (Bats) 53

But Does Springsteen Help Move Pianos? 55

Talk About "Strange," Talk About "Crazy" 58

10 Reasons Kansans Endure David Letterman 60

But Was Gomez Addams "30something"? 63

Come On, Deeb! Stomp Farrah's Head, Man! 65

What's One More Disgusting, Twisted, Offensive Movie? 68
But Pity John Irving's Weak-Stomached Readers..............70
"Just Call Me Jim, Jessica . . . " 73
Is Kitty Kelley Ruining Fame?............................76

If Elected . . .

This Isn't Quite How Ted Koppel Does It...........................80
Now May I Ask You This, Sir: *Huh?* 83
How to Win Elections – and Pick Up Women 85
Being Nice to Donna Rice......................................88
May I Speak to a World Leader, Please?...........................91
Play the Primary Game; Everyone's a Winner! 93
Go, Grads! Go Be Happy and Harmless!............................96
How Would Media Handle Armageddon? 99
Getting Away From It All......................................101

I ❤ Kansas (Really!)

VISIT EXCITING KANSAS! SEE MOODY COW!.......106
Real Kansas Men Never Even Heard of Quiche 108
Love Those Real Kansas Women......................................111
Where Were You June 22, 1989?!? 114
So Kansas Is Flat; What of It?............................116
Jet-Setters Just Love the Kansas State Fair 119
Even in Dodge City, "The Sun Also Rises".....................122
Welcome to the 20th Century, Kansas! 125

Please Don't Quit, Santa

How to Tell if It's Love 130

Valentines You Won't Find in Stores 132
How to Make Labor Day *Work* 135
For the Man or Woman Who Has Everything... 137
What if We Have to Replace Santa?.............................140
Saying Thank You Isn't Always Easy 142

Mind if I Get Personal?

Which to Have? Kids or a Dog?.............................148
Pushy? Who? This Little League Dad?.............................150
Who Says Father Knows Best? 152
Are Dads Better or Worse Today?.............................155
Are You Surviving Your Teenagers?.............................158
Unhappy Birthday to You, Unhappy Birthday to You... ..160
Midlife Crisis – or Coffee Nerves? 163
I Love . . . I Hate 166
Good Neighbor Jack.............................168
Mom 171

Fun (Ahem) & Games

About Those W's, L's, O's, M's and Dingers 176
Moral: Never Punch a Marshmallow Salesman.............178
Maybe Woody Hayes Wasn't Ideal Role Model 181
The Raging Creature of Indiana Basketball 183
Once Upon a Time in Kansas.............................185
Was Wilt Just Afraid of the Dark?.............................188

The Smoking Section

What Kind of Fool Are Smokers?.............................194
Quitting Smoking Is Like Being Dead, Only Worse.........197

Fat City, No; Fat Country, Yes 199
Shocking Stuff Women Should Know About Men!..........201
"This Is the Merkle Car, Bambi Speaking" 204
Jeannette Ewertz Isn't Somebody Else – Honest!.............207
Torture, 20th-Century Style................................209
No Music to Discuss Miss Manners by............................212
Ban Those Babies! Ban Those Babies! 214
I'm Late! I'm Late! For . . . Ah, Who Cares? 217
Cats Must Be Morons...220
Arf! Arf! Arf! Bark! Aarrroooooo! 222
So Go Have a Lousy Day!.................................225

BEWARE OF THE REALITY

"If a mommy can make a deal for her test-tube baby, how long will it be before a good hotshot attorney comes along who persuades a court that a nice young couple who are really financially strapped should be allowed to sell their cute, lovable, housebroken 9-year-old?"

1975

Is Earth Going Crazy? How About It, Doc?

February 28, 1979

Probably because of the hectic holiday season, no one seemed to notice that the Earth sneaked off the other day to see a psychiatrist in a neighboring solar system.

"I've got problems, Doctor," Earth said, starting to quiver so nervously and violently from pole to pole that it spilled some ocean on the heavens.

"Ah, but we all haf our proplums, Earth," said the psychiatrist, a very advanced planet with a goatee.

"Not like mine," Earth moaned, its voice and continents trembling. "Eternity is getting me down, Doctor. Sometimes I think I'm going to go completely berserk and fly off my axis. I don't know if I can even make it through one more year."

"There, there, Earth. Chust take it easy ant relax. Eternity is chust somesing we planets must learn to live vit. Ant it can't be all zat bad. Maybe is somesing physical, hawh? Or maybe chust somesing you ate?"

"Well, part of it is definitely physical, Doctor, but it's the stress I can't take anymore."

"Hmmm. And vot are zee physical symptoms?"

"Droughts. Floods. Migraine earthquakes at all hours. Dizzy spells. The chills. Heat waves. Congestion."

"But zose are chust sings lots of planets haf to live vit, Earth. Zose sings come and go away."

"But there's one more thing, Doctor."

"Yah? And vot is dot?"

"I hate to admit it. I'm . . . I'm so ashamed."

2

"Nonsense! It can't be all zat bad. Hawh?"

"Well, Doctor, I'm . . . well, uh, I'm, I'm *inhabited!*"

"Oh my Got! You poor ting. Vot are you inhabited by?"

"Human beings – among other things."

"And vot do zeese human beings do, Earth?"

"Well, they're tiny little two-legged creatures who crawl, walk, run, fall down, scamper, scurry, dart, jump, clamber, turn somersaults. . . . "

"But zey sound furry amusing, Earth! Vhere's your sense of humor?"

"Sense of humor? Ha! These humans also blow up parts of me, burn me, dig holes in me, tear out my trees, try to suffocate me with concrete, pour poison in my water, pollute my atmosphere, use up all my oil – I think they want to destroy me!"

"Aha! Now ve are getting somevhere. Paranoia!"

"Paranoia my axis! These humans have bombed me! And they've even had races to see who could come up with the most devastating bomb! And now, lately, my Iran has flared up and irritated my United States, which has bombs!"

"Dot's chust turrble, Earth. I neffer heard such turrble proplums, so I sink you muss be imagining sings. Vot vee muss do is locate zee root of your proplums. Vhen do you sink your proplums began, Earth? Do you remember, hawh?"

"Sure, that's easy. In the beginning, God created the heavens and me. Then on the *sixth* day . . . "

Just How Good Were the Good Old Days?

December 23, 1987

Even the very least-informed, hazy-brained slugs among us know that times have changed a bit since the dearly beloved, if painfully over-nostalgia-fied 1950s.

But I wonder if younger people, in particular, realize how radical some of the changes have been.

Being the unstoppably helpful sort, what I have done here today is come up with some actual figures, some real live numbers, to create a unique comparison of the '50s and the '80s.

What I've done is estimate, roughly, on a scale of zero to 10 the probability of certain things happening in the '50s and in the '80s, with zero meaning there would be no chance of something happening in that decade, and 10 meaning something would be guaranteed to happen.

Older people, check me out. Younger people, rejoice at how much society has loosened up. . . .

• The chances in the 1950s you had been married to the same person your whole life: 8.

The 1980s chances you have been married to Elizabeth Taylor or Zsa Zsa Gabor, among others, at least once each: 8.

• 1950s chances you knew of a store that had air conditioning: 2.

1950s chances you knew somebody personally who had air conditioning in his or her home: 1.

1980s chances you have air conditioning in your house, car, van, garage, doghouse, child's dollhouse and jogging

4

shorts: 8.

- 1950s chances of students being mugged at the average school: zero.

1980s chances of students being mugged on the school grounds: 6.

1980s chances of students being nuked on the school grounds: 2.

- 1950s chances of seeing an actress' knees in a movie: 5.

1980s chances of seeing nudity at home on TV: 10.

- 1950s chances of your being on a TV show: 1.

1980s chances of your being the host of a TV show: 9.

- 1950s chances you knew somebody who did drugs: zero.

1980s chances you are doing 25 years in prison right now for smuggling drugs from Colombia: 5.

- 1950s chances you knew someone who had plastic surgery who hadn't been in a horrible, disfiguring accident: zero.

1980s chances you will wake up some day and see after the bandages are removed that you are starting to resemble Michael Jackson: 7.

- 1950s chances of a girl under 13 having pierced ears: 1.

1980s chances of a girl under 13 going to a rock concert with a safety pin in her nose and wearing a negligee: 3.

- 1950s chances of your 10-year-old daughter arriving home with her ears newly pierced and wearing gaudy earrings: zero.

1980s chances of your 10-year-old son arriving home with an ear newly pierced and wearing an earring: 7.

- 1950s chances of seeing someone in church not wearing a suit and tie or best dress: zero.

1980s chances of seeing someone in church wearing their best jogging suit and sneakers: 6.

- 1950s chances of a TV star who is on the air phoning you to chat: zero.

1980s chances of David Letterman calling you up: 9.

- 1950s chances of a sixth-grader being able to locate, name and give the capitals of all the states: 9.

1980s chances of a sixth-grader being able to locate the United States on a globe and name Washington, D.C., as its capital: 4.

- 1950s chances your small town had a movie theater: 10.

1980s chances your small town has a movie theater – that is now used as a depot for the Greyhound bus route: 10.

- 1950s chances you lived in a beautiful, modern $30,000 home: 5.

1980s chances you live in a tiny, dumpy, ancient $65,000 home: 8.

- 1950s chances I knew what I was talking about: 5.

1980s chances: Uh, uh, uh . . .

———

The Devil and Oral Roberts

February 22, 1987

I don't get it.

The devil personally tries to strangle Granville Oral Roberts, 69, of Tulsa, Okla., and not only are people scoffing about the alleged attack, but my own ordinarily sensitive, conscientious newspaper buried this historic, phenomenal news way back on a comic page, of all places, in the People column.

Consider the indignity of this.

Here the devil, according to Oral, tried to wring his neck, and where does the story end up but on a page that carries The Far Side, Funky Winkerbean and the continuing adventures of Madonna and Sean!

Isn't that an insult to both Oral . . . and the devil?

At least it was the *lead* item in that People column.

But it's just a good thing Vanna White didn't do anything important that day, like reveal her philosophy of life or bring out her own brand of salad dressing, or you know what would have happened to Oral's story. It would have been bumped to Item No. 2, and the whole pagewide headline would have gone to the Grand Dame of Game Shows.

Personally, I think Oral's extraordinary story should have been spread across the top of Page 1A with screaming headlines so towering, so imposing, they would have frightened the National Enquirer: Devil Tries to Strangle Oral Roberts! Wife's Quick Actions Save Evangelist!

I mean, come on, now. You have to admit it isn't every day that Satan tries to strangle somebody, or is even accused of trying.

Maybe the story didn't get better play in our paper because it wasn't local.

If the devil had tried to strangle, say, a city commissoner, that might have made Page 1A.

In fact, just imagine how such a story would have been handled, starting with a major news conference:

"What exactly did the devil look like, Mayor Casado?"

"Well, uh, it was awfully dark, you know. And I didn't have my glasses on."

"Are you sure it wasn't a burglar disguised as the devil?"

"Well, if so, the police should be looking for a man with orange eyes that glow."

"Did he say anything to you? Make any threats? Offer

7

you any good Faustian deals? Talk to you about your soul or something?"

"No. He was just strangling me."

I just hope the Robertses had the presence of mind to report this alleged crime to the Tulsa police right away.

After all, it's one thing if the devil is after our souls, but when he gets so overanxious he starts getting physical and trying to snuff us out before our time with his own bare hands, or hooves, well, I just think he's getting completely out of line and going entirely too far in this apparently escalating battle between good and evil.

I wonder what all the other big TV evangelists think about this. Do they consider it presumptuous of Oral to claim the devil singled him out to strangle? Are they jealous because the devil might not consider them important enough, or strong enough competition, to try to personally wring their necks, too?

I don't mean to be irreverent here. You know me. But you have to admit that Oral Roberts has raised almost as many eyebrows as dollars, having claimed he's seen a 900-foot Jesus, and by claiming God told him if he doesn't come up with $8 million by March 31, he will die.

That's why I'd like to propose that Oral allow a reporter to stay with him at all times from now on through April to be a witness if anything rather unusual happens again. And I would consider this assignment myself.

Imagine a chance to interview the devil.

"Tell me, Satan – May I call you Satan? – If you were a tree, what kind would you be?"

Talk about a major scoop. Barbara Walters would never get over it.

Waiting for McMahon
and $10 Million

September 22, 1986

It – he – was really beginning to get to me.

Who was this young man who was always sitting on one of the benches in front of The Eagle every day, all day long, for the last two weeks?

Every time I walked by, there he was, sitting with a gym-type bag on the sidewalk beside him, and he was always unfailingly friendly.

I couldn't take it anymore.

Late Thursday afternoon, I plopped down beside him, introduced myself and said I was going nuts, wondering what he was doing there.

"I'm making a statement to the world," he said.

"What kind of statement?"

"I'm not sure what it is yet," he said.

OK. That sounds a lot like me. I asked his name.

"Arthur J. Barker."

Age?

"I'm 27 years young. And I am going to be the 20th-century evangelist. I've been here since Monday, September the 8th," he said. "I stay at the mission. I sleep in a laundry room. I stayed two nights with friends. And two nights I was right here."

A nice-looking, well-dressed woman walked by.

"Hi!" Barker said, brightly.

The woman picked up her pace, eyes straight ahead.

Barker grinned, beat his chest and exclaimed, "Woooo-oooo!"

9

Arthur Barker wore a MICHIGAN T-shirt and gray dress slacks. Some days his eyes were badly bloodshot, but this day he looked rested. His brown hair was combed neatly, and he was clean-shaven.

I asked what his plans were.

"My plans? To sit here until Ed McMahon shows up and blesses me with $10 million."

"Why would Ed McMahon do that?"

"For winning the Publishers Clearinghouse Sweepstakes!" Barker said, sounding annoyed with me. "Do you know what faith is? I have faith in God's promise for a miracle."

How would Ed McMahon find him?

"I'm not gonna worry about it! Details! I can't worry about 'em!"

But what if it gets cold and Ed McMahon hasn't come yet?

"I can't worry about it! Doing this is gonna bless me."

A car pulled up to the curb. It was about 6 p.m. Barker said he had to go. A friend was going to let him stay at his place.

The next morning when I arrived at work about 7 a.m., there Barker was, as always, and we picked right up where we left off.

"I talk to a lot of people here," he said. "I let them know I'm waiting for Ed McMahon.

"If I done this back when I was a worldly person," he said, "I would have thought I was crazy. But now I'm a servant of the living God."

He burst into laughter.

"Some people think I'm looney tunes. But when Ed McMahon drives up and gives me $10 million, people are gonna think, 'If that dummy could do that with faith, I can do it, too!' "

Barker said he's from a small town in Kansas. Dropped out of high school his senior year and ended up joining the Marines as an alternative to going to jail for some trouble he got into.

He said that after he got out of the Marines, he was hit by a car and crippled badly. He had to wear a brace on his leg, he said, but exactly one year ago today, he just took it off and was healed through faith.

Another woman walked by.

"When I get my $10 million, gonna be a lot of women who'd like to be my wife," Barker said. "Ain't none of 'em gonna (take advantage of) me, though. I'm gonna wait till Father tells me which one."

His mood darkening unexpectedly, he said, "I'm so mad at the world I can't even cry. But someday I'm gonna lock myself up in a room and cry and cry for four days!"

Then, brightly, he said, "You know what I think? I think today's the day!

"You know what I think?" he repeated. "Every day's the day!"

He roared with laughter.

I wished Arthur Barker luck.

"You gonna write about this now?" he asked. "Or are you gonna wait until Ed McMahon comes? That will really be a story."

Hang in there, Arthur. A lot of the rest of us kind of have our own Ed McMahons we're waiting for, too.

(NOTE: Arthur J. Barker is not the man's real name.)

This Coupon Worth $5 Toward a Nice Divorce

August 26, 1977

Lawyers can advertise now. The Supreme Court said so.

That's not supposed to mean that legal counsel will soon be a commodity as cherished by the consumer as cat food, deodorant and mouthwash. But who knows?

I doubt, too, that lawyers will soon be running discount coupons in newspapers, i.e. "This coupon worth $5 toward a divorce." But who knows?

Certain guidelines have been established, presumably to keep lawyers' advertising from becoming as tacky as most other advertising, but those guidelines look awfully flexible from where I sit.

That's why I'm considering zipping out to Los Angeles to open an advertising agency for lawyers. I'll be ready when California permits TV commercials for lawyers.

With any luck, my first commercial will star Zsa Zsa Gabor, if I can catch her between husbands.

The commercial will open with her lounging in a mansion. She'll be dressed regally and wearing enough sparklers to open her own diamond mine.

"Hello, darlinks. Maybe you are askink yourself, 'How does a poor little sing like me manage to get by and live like zis between husbands, wiz today's cost of liffing being vut it is?'

"I have a mansion, a Lake Michigan-sized svimming pool, a tennis court and a private airport in my back yard. I have luxury cars to match all zee outfits in my wardrobe, and I have enough spending money to buy Great Britain.

"How do I do eet? I owe eet all to my law firm, Leech and McTick, zee best divorce attorneys in the business. Zey have handled three million divorces – not all of zem mine, ha ha! – so zey know what zey are doink!

"And if zey don't give you full satisfaction, zey vill give you your ex-husband back!

"Now, because there is such a rapid turnover of spouses anymore, Leech and McTick are making special bonus offer.

"If you let zem handle your next three divorces, zey vill handle your fourth divorce at no cost, whatsoever.

"For furzer information, contact zem immediately. And tell zem Zsa Zsa sends you!"

•

Or maybe I could get the possibly over-married Mickey Rooney. I can see him coming on a commercial, wearing nothing but a barrel.

"Hi. Do you want to know why I'm standing here on television wearing nothing but a barrel?

"I'll tell you why. It's because my ex-wives got everything I ever owned, plus all my income, in divorce settlements.

"What is my ex-wives' secret? Simple. Good divorce lawyers. And when it comes to divorces, there are just no attorneys better than Pincher, Pincher and Pincher.

"Now! This month, and this month only, Pincher, Pincher and Pincher are making a special introductory offer to all new clients, charging just one half their normal fee.

"So act fast and take advantage of this once-in-a-lifetime offer while it's still good. If you've been thinking about divorcing your spouse for years but have been putting it off for one reason or another, this is the opportunity you've been waiting for.

"And even if you're happily married and have never considered getting a divorce, think it over. Phone Pincher,

Pincher and Pincher right now, and let them send you their free brochure called 'How to Turn a Happy, Solid Marriage Into a Successful, Highly Profitable Divorce Settlement.'

"Remember! You may be happily married today, but you have to think of your future and plan ahead.

"Why wait one, five or 10 years for your marriage to go sour? Why not act now, while this offer is still good, and divorce your spouse while you're still young enough to enjoy the property settlement and the alimony?

"So, for the best divorce deal in town, call Pincher, Pincher and Pincher, the law firm with a heart!"

———

Remember When Selling Kiddies Was Illegal?

April 12, 1987

Why fight it? I guess I just might as well resign myself to the horrifying, painful truth that I have become hopelessly, prematurely old-fashioned, a regular old fuddy-duddy, a cultural antique, a reluctant relic of ancient times.

You want to know what a sorry old fogey I am?

I still think bell-bottom pants are pretty cool-looking; I am sometimes troubled by all the clean-cut, short-haired young people I see, even though I wasn't even a hippie myself; and if you can believe this, I really hate it when mothers sell their babies.

What can I say? I guess the world has begun to pass me by.

It boggles my mind that any civilized authority would even consider allowing the sale of an artificially daddied baby, let alone approve it, thus creating the Baby M mess not even Solomon could solve.

14

Yep, all you young whippersnappers. Times have changed a bit.

Tarnation, would you believe it used to be illegal to sell babies?

That's how backward and uptight society was in my day.

Heck, you would have thought that human life was sacred or that a family's flesh and blood had some silly significance the way people looked down their noses and called the cops whenever any enterprising entrepreneurs tried to make a buck by selling a child.

So these are exciting times. Now that women are allowed to reap a profit peddling their flesh and blood, what next?

If a mommy can make a deal for her baby, how long will it be before a good hotshot attorney comes along who persuades a court that a nice young couple who are really financially strapped should be allowed to sell their cute, lovable, housebroken 9-year-old?

And then how long would it be before the kid market was absolutely glutted with teenagers, the Classifieds jammed with ads like this:

FOR SALE – Male, 15. 6-1, 129 pounds. Eats like canary. Hates loud music. Hates TV. Likes to read in his room, do dishes, vacuum, mow lawn, take out trash. $1,500 or best offer.

False advertising might be a problem. So I suppose we could expect legislation requiring all contracts for sales of kids to include escape clauses allowing the purchasers 30-day trials before the sales are final.

But imagine what might be ahead in the baby market.

Couples may shop for a designated mother simply to avoid the general ordeal, restrictions and inconveniences that go with pregnancy, especially if, say, they would like to have a baby next January but it would conflict with a ski trip they'd like to take in December.

Yep, folks. Why not just buy a baby? Look in the Yellow Pages under Surrogate Mothers, check around, look for the best bargain.

But, please! Let's hear nothing about such transactions being a sign that our country has sunk into complete moral bankruptcy. I mean, hey, baby: These are the '80s! Get with it. In fact, you might just want to buy a little tyke, even if you don't want or need one, just to show your neighbors how totally trendy you are!

Some women could even make "surrogating" a career. A sturdy, dedicated designated mother might earn $15,000 to $30,000 a year mostly in the comfort of her own home, just watching soaps and kind of functioning as a baby machine or baby factory.

Newspaper birth announcements might appear in the business section.

And imagine stores' advertisements for surrogate mommies:

Mona. Age 24. Natural hair color mousy brown. 5-7. 131 pounds. Medium build. IQ 109. Moderately athletic. Bats right, throws right. Voice high-pitched and slightly shrieky but sort of charming in its way. Strong hands. Excellent teeth. SPECIAL PRICE THIS WEEK ONLY – $18,700! (All sales of mothers' babies final.)

After that, I guess we could expect Surrogate Mother Agencies to open like real estate agencies and pet stores, with catchy names like Rent-a-Mom, Superkids Inc., Womb Central, Hire-a-Mommy and Birthco.

But do you know when this will be completely out of hand?

When somebody like Yves St. Laurent or Calvin Klein figures out how to produce "designer babies."

Maybe they'd better stop this nonsense before it's too late, huh?

If it isn't already.

———

Dear Rex Humbard: PLEASE READ THIS!!!

April 17, 1983

DEAR REX HUMBARD:

THIS OPEN LETTER TO YOU IS URGENT! IF YOU DO NOT READ IT, THE ENTIRE FLORIDA ORANGE CROP MAY BE LOST THIS YEAR, THE SPACE PROGRAM MAY SKID TO A HALT, AND IT MIGHT BREAK MY DEAR FAMILY'S HEART!

But don't panic, Rex. Even though I came on a little strong there, using your own techniques to grab your attention, you can relax. I am not going to ask you for money.

Rex? The reason I'm writing is to let you know about the very surprising reaction I got to a column I wrote last week.

The column was about that letter you sent out, asking people to "save" your TV ministry by sending you amounts of money up to $100 and even $200. Mostly, I just quoted your letter before wondering, in conclusion, whether you really know what pressures you are putting on people who don't have much, if any, money.

YOU MUST READ THIS PARAGRAPH (to use another device of yours):

I expected to take a lot of heat for that column, Rex. But, surprisingly, the large majority of people who responded commended me "for having the courage" to write such a column. And some who said they agreed with the column also said they are on your mailing list.

More specifically, one man wondered why it is so important for you to be on TV time and time again each week, if you can't afford it. After all, he said, it's not like this is a heathen country. There are plenty of ministers of all faiths around who not only would be happy to make house calls but who would gladly do it without asking for any money, and no doubt none would have the audacity to ask for sums like $100 from people who obviously can't afford it.

Then some people seem to have the impression, Rex, that you are caught up in a peculiar, self-perpetuating operation that consists mostly of your asking people to send you money to stay on the air so you can stay on the air and keep asking people to send you money.

You may be the most godly of men, Rex, and no doubt you do good works. But some people seem convinced that if God really wants you to stay on television, he'll keep you there without putting additional hardships on people who can barely afford to pay their own bills, let alone help you pay yours.

Two of the few people who didn't appreciate my previous column about you, Rex, told me I'm going to hell for writing it. One of those persons argued that you aren't *forcing* anybody to send you money.

But you sort of do try to use "force," don't you, Rex? Because your letters use people's own faith against them, in a way. You suggest that if people's faith is indeed genuine, and they want to keep souls from burning through "eternity in a *literal* Pit of Fire" (I'm quoting you there, Rex), they will send you the sum requested and trust God to take care of their electric bill, or whatever.

Moreover, you write such things as, "You may not have

the $100 to give, but I pray that God will lead you to where you can get $100. . . . "

I don't know if that's playing fair, Rex. Because my guess is the elderly are the most susceptible to your pleas, aren't they? That's why con artists tend to prey on the elderly, you know. Because they're more trusting, more pliable, so much more vulnerable.

A few people in their 70s and 80s phoned me. It was kind of sad.

I even went out to the house of one older woman who is not only quite disillusioned with you, Rex, but very upset.

She said, "He (you) was on TV (several months ago), beggin' for money, and he said send whatever you can, even if it was only one dollar. Well, I had a dollar bill and I sent it, and he sent me *another* letter asking for money to help teach the little children in South America the word God, so I sent (another small sum). And he *kept* sending me letters, asking for money, and I didn't have any! Then he sent me a letter saying he had to have $10 for an emergency, so I got it, but I wrote a note with it. I said, 'Don't write me anymore for money. I have too many medical expenses!' "

After which she received a request for $25, followed soon after by a request for $15. And then she saw my column, and phoned me nervously.

Rex? Since writing that column, I've seen stories saying your ministry has been "saved" from your creditors. For some reason, I wasn't surprised.

And I saw one other item about you in a newspaper recently, too.

It said you have purchased $1.4 million in real estate this year.

What for, Rex? To build low-rent housing for some of the people off whom you have lived so long yourself?

How Long Should Miracles Last?

February 21, 1990

Do miracles, true miracles, fizzle out? Wilt like week-old roses? Turn sour with time? Go stale? Have an expiration date?

Are there partial miracles?

Temporary miracles?

Four months ago, in late October, two professed miracle-workers, Charles and Frances Hunter, popped into Wichita to sing peppy religious tunes, chat in "tongues" and heal people.

They set up their traveling healing show, their moving miracle-working shop, at the Kansas Coliseum.

Always one to enjoy a joke, I went to watch.

I'm still don't know what I saw. But it sure looked to the skeptical eye a lot like mass hocus-pocus. One thing it was not was funny. A lot of desperate people were there, some terminally ill. During the evening, many people claimed to be healed – mainly, it seemed, people with aches and pains and stiffness of joints. But many were not healed – especially those who came in wheelchairs.

What I did was randomly pick out three people who said they experienced some degree of healing, and write about them.

Then this month, I got back in touch with the same three people to see how their healing is holding up.

Leona Bunch, 74, says she still feels better than she did before she went out to the healing program.

"I feel all right yet," she said. "I'm still walking better

20

than before."

But Mrs. Bunch has cancer and arthritis and continues to use a wheelchair sometimes.

Ruth Tweet says the intense pain she had for years from tendinitis is much less severe. But she said it had eased up even before the healing. And she says she still wears braces on her legs.

Ruth's mother, Kay, said, "She's much better. The pain isn't totally gone, but she's much, much better. The Lord does heal."

But it was Frank Zalewski who seemed to experience the greatest transformation.

A degenerative disc disease in his neck had caused Zalewski such pain that he hadn't been able to bowl or do woodworking, two things he has always loved, for years.

But at the faith-healing session, he and his wife, Gloria, were amazed and ecstatic when his pain immediately disappeared. And, soon after I wrote about him, he resumed bowling and woodworking.

Not having bowled since 1983, Zalewski, who had been a 175-average bowler, joined a league late last year and averaged in the 160s.

But when I talked to Zalewski for a second time in recent weeks, the pain was back. He said the pain came back recently while he was bowling.

"It hurts more now than it did before," he said.

He faults his doctor, not the healers, for the return of the pain.

He said his doctor should have advised him against bowling.

"I shouldn't have bowled," Zalewski said. "Right now, I can't do anything (including woodworking) that has to do with lifting."

You might say Zalewski still believes in miracles – but

not very much.

"All it (the healing) got rid of was the pain," he said, "but it didn't replace the disc in my neck, and that's the real problem. I didn't think it was going to keep working. But if they'd (the healers) given me a new disc, I'd make history and you'd really have a story."

I asked Zalewski's doctor what he thought about the Hunters' healing show, where they seemed to dispense miracles like Band-Aids.

The doctor wasn't inclined to say much.

"I certainly believe in anything that works," he said, slyly.

So. Is Frank Zalewski disillusioned with the healing Hunters?

"I'd go out again if they come back," he said. "It's not their fault. I shouldn't have been bowling."

———

Ain't You Seen Nothin' Yet, Officers?

October 7, 1984

News item – *Two Wichita taverns were closed temporarily after undercover officers reported that a dancer in one had worn a see-through garment and a dancer in the other exposed her chest.*

Today's episode of this season's hot new series, "Vice Guys," opens in The Flesh Pit, a typically sad Wichita tavern. On the outside, a portable sign exaggerates, EXOTIC DANCING GIRLS – 3 TO MIDNITE!!!

Inside, undercover vice officers Lumox and

McClandestine, dressed in street clothes, sit at a table near a small dance platform.

On the platform, a bored-looking young performer seems to be standing and chewing gum vigorously. But if you look closely, you can detect she is sort of dancing.

"Having a good time, Lumox?" McClandestine asks.

"I told you to stop asking me that! We're working, you know. We're not supposed to be having a good time. It would be unprofessional to have a good time while we're on duty drinking beer, eating pretzels and beef jerkies, and staking out scantily clad dancer individuals."

"Well, like they say, a little hard work never hurt anybody."

"Besides, that's no dancer individual up there. That's a zombie. Somebody ought to check her pulse. She's probably dead and just continues chewing gum out of force of habit."

"Don't get world-weary on me, Lumox. People are supposed to enjoy their work. Even us. Oh, waitress individual! Two more beers!"

Lumox sighs, "I'd rather be home watching TV. Wake me when the vice starts."

"Do you know Krupke made an arrest last night? He said this individual was a real looker. He said he watched her for three hours just to be absolutely positive she was guilty of toplessness."

"The man is dedicated."

The song on the jukebox ends, and a new dancer, Vikki, comes on. She is a beauty who writhes and bounces with much talent and abandon.

"She looks suspicious to me," McClandestine whispers.

"10-4," Lumox says. "Don't let her out of your sight."

Lumox goes to the men's room and talks into his police radio.

"We have a suspect under surveillance – female, about

5-7, 115 pounds, with gorgeous – er, long blond hair, and she's wearing a halter, a cute little skirt but, well, mostly just sequins."

Lumox hurries back to the table to help his partner watch the suspect.

"Need some help here?" Lumox asks.

"I appreciate your esprit de corps," Mac says.

"My reward is in the fact the good citizens of Wichita must sleep better knowing we're out here protecting them from female individuals who show their chests."

Before long, Vikki expresses herself artistically via her chest.

"Stand by," Lumox whispers to Mac.

Two hours later, after Vikki has danced nine more times bare-chested, and it's almost closing time, Lumox nods. Immediately, Vikki and the manager are apprehended. The tavern is shut down.

Afterward, Lumox goes home, opens a beer, plops down by the TV, and looks in the Cable Guide to see if any good "R" movies with maybe a little more than toplessness are coming up. He reads . . .

Aphrodite (Nudity); Black Emanuelle (Nudity); Confessions of a Driving Instructor (Nudity); Emily ("Koo Stark experiences the joys of womanhood as the sensual, fun-loving Emily"); Eros America 3 ("Visit a legal bordello and a beauty contest that bares all in an evening of fare for the discriminating adult"); Fiona ("Fiona has an insatiable sexual appetite, far naughtier than ever imagined"); Humanoids from the Deep ("Sex-starved aquatic mutants rise from the ocean's depths to mate with women"); Lady on the Bus (Nudity – "Sonja Braga encounters sensuous experiences on a bus ride through Rio"); Private School (Nudity – "Plenty of pranks") . . .

Eyes gleaming, Lumox flicks on the Showtime channel.

This Is Your Captain Speaking; Shall We Pray?

August 21, 1981

As I drove to the airport Wednesday to grope around for an illuminating story for Sunday about the aftermath of the air traffic controllers' strike, I didn't know what to expect out there.

My imagination was way ahead of me, though, as I envisioned absolute chaos in the control tower. Something like this:

"Look out, Braniff Flight 425! Look out!"

"Hang a sharp left, United 366! And I do mean sharp!"

"Oh, my God! Not again."

"Better luck next time, Ralph."

"Now, now. You'll get the hang of it before long. Won't he, Bill?"

"Aw-oh. TWA 248? Duck! Duck!"

"Dive, Continental 411! Dive, man!"

"Whew! That was close."

"Hi, guys, I'm Herbie. They just sent me up from Air Traffic Control 101 to help. Hey, what are all those little blips on the screen? They're really neat. Like a Space Invaders video game. Where do I put my quarter to play?"

"Get outta here, you idiot!"

"Wichita? Wichita? This is Delta 924 out of St. Louis. Can you hear me? I think you must have made some sort of mistake. I seem to have landed on Highway 54. Can you see me from the tower? What should I do now?"

"I see you, 924. Nice landing. Now just pull out over into the right lane and hang a right at the second traffic light.

25

You can't miss the airport from there. It's the place with all the pickets walking around in front."

"Hola? Hola? Donde esta Mexico? Donde esta Mexico, por favor?"

"Hey, guys? Anybody up here speak French? I think we got a French plane overhead somehow."

"I think the pilot's talking Spanish, Charlie."

"Whatever. I think he's landing in the wrong country."

"Here, let me talk to him. *Amigo? Amigo? Esta* Weecheeta! Kansas! United States-os! *Vaya con* south!"

"OK, Pan Am 511, you are clear for takeoff, now. But for God's sakes, man, hurry!"

"Control tower? Hello, Hello? This is Air Midwest Flight 666 from Dodge City. Correct me if I'm wrong, but I would swear you brought me down in the Towne West shopping center parking lot."

"Don't hassle me, 666. I'm new at this and doing the best I can."

"Well, look, tower. As long as I'm over here, do you mind if I run in and buy a new shirt? The one I'm wearing is soaked."

"Ummm, OK, 666. But lock the plane while you're in there, and don't forget where you parked. The last thing I need is some airline on my back for losing a planeful of passengers in a parking lot. And those planes are expensive, you know. They'd probably take it out of my paycheck."

"Control tower, control tower, this is Pan Am 808. Can you read me? Can you read me?"

"Loud and clear, 808. What's up – heh, heh."

"I was just kinda wondering. Is this Omaha?"

"Sorry, 808. This is Wichita."

"Are you sure? I'd swear the tower in Denver said Omaha was this way."

"I swear, man. This is Wichita."

"Hmmm. Well, I guess I'll just have to keep looking. It has to be around here somewhere, I imagine."

"Tower! Tower! Please come in! Please! This is American Flight 321, and I'm Sally the stewardess!"

"Hi, Sally. I'm Benny. What can I do for you?"

"Help! Our pilot and co-pilot heard you guys down there talking, and they panicked and bailed out! Now there's nobody up here who can fly the plane! What should I do?"

"Hmmm. Could you hold for just a sec, Sally? Good. Uh, Herbie? Herbie? Come back over here, will you?"

"What is it, Benny?"

"Here. It's for you."

———

The Most Outrageous Ticket Ever Written?

August 7, 1987

Hold it! Stop the presses! This could be it. The greatest, the most outrageous traffic ticket in history. What an all-time doozy.

It was a Saturday afternoon in Wichita. The wedding and the reception at the church were over. Mark, 21, and Margie, 18, hurried out to their '76 Toyota Corolla, where they were surprised and amused to see what Mark's brother and some friends had done to the windows.

"JUST MARRIED" was scrawled across the rear window. Lips were drawn on side windows. And squiggly lines were all over the windshield.

Bride and groom hopped in the car. They didn't have far to go. They were headed for the Hilton East to spend the night, and the next day they would leave the car behind and go to Dallas for their honeymoon. So off they drove toward the Hilton.

Then it was, near Lincoln and Edgemoor, that a police car, overhead lights flashing, came charging up behind them.

"At first," Mark said, "I thought, 'Oh, God, what am I doing wrong?' I wasn't speeding. I wasn't driving all over the place. I was confused why he was pulling me over."

The police officer was, it seems, just doing his duty, keeping Wichita's streets safe from newlyweds.

The officer stopped Mark and Margie (not their real names; they've had enough embarrassment for one week) because Mark's view was obstructed by all those squiggles on the windshield.

"I won't deny there were a lot of squiggles on the windshield, but I could see good enough," Mark said. "I said to him, 'Everybody does that on their wedding day.' He said he could tolerate the writing, but not all the other stuff."

The officer's devotion to duty paid extra dividends. When he asked Mark for his driver's license, Mark realized it was in one of his suitcases in the back of the car and not handy.

So, while the new bride sat there in her wedding gown in the car in the sizzling Saturday heat, the determined officer invited Mark back into his squad car, where, Mark said, Officer Killjoy spent about 15 minutes running a radio check on him and writing up a ticket for driving with an obstructed view and without a driver's license in his possession.

"I felt he could have just said, 'Let's get it wiped off, and then you can continue on your way,' " Mark said. "But he just wrote up a ticket. And I didn't give him a hard time."

The officer told Mark to clean the window before driving on, and left. So Mark borrowed some glass cleaner and a rag from a nearby restaurant and cleaned the windshield. Ah, such honeymoon memories.

Mark's father, who lives in Dallas, phoned me early the following Monday. He had been here for the wedding and was still furious.

"I don't mean to sound unreasonable," he began, "but this was nonsense! I understand the windshield view was obstructed. But I am so aggravated that this officer would embarrass and humiliate these kids and ruin their wedding day.

"I could have understood him stopping my son and telling him he needed to clean off the windshield, but he embarrassed them, scared them and made (Mark) sit in the police car while his new bride was left sitting there. I am so mad I could file a suit against the officer."

Because Mark's father also complained to the Wichita Police Department's Internal Affairs Division, which could result in a departmental investigation, "Officer Killjoy's" superiors were reluctant to discuss the ticket with me.

And the officer himself, through his supervisor, Lt. Nolan Spruill, said he didn't wish to be interviewed.

Spruill said, "(The officer) said he would leave this up to the courts. He just said the windshield was very obscured, and it was impossible to see."

The fine facing Mark for an obstructed view is $25. There will be no other fine if he produces his driver's license within 10 days.

Mark could, of course, take the ticket to court.

"I don't want him to have to go to court," Mark's father said. "I want something done about this outrage. That's why I called Internal Affairs."

About the ticket, written by one of his officers, Capt. John Hershberger did say, "Unfortunately, there's nothing in the city ordinances that exempts you on your wedding day."

But I don't think Mark and Margie wanted anything as grand or remarkable as an exemption or special treatment.

Just some common sense, simple understanding and reasonable, non-outrageous treatment probably would have satisfied them just fine.

(Soon after this column appeared, the chief of police dismissed the ticket.)

———

Danny Wants Back in Prison – for Good

September 3, 1989

And you thought you'd heard it all. Danny, 26, wants to go to prison. He wants to be deposited in prison, locked up, and he doesn't care if they throw the key away.

Unfortunately for Danny, of course, prisons aren't much like hotels. When you get in the mood to spend the rest of your life in prison, you can't just make a reservation and go. MasterCard and Visa do you no good. Slipping a warden a twenty won't help.

To get into prison, you have to do something pretty nasty and risky, like make a big withdrawal from a bank with a gun instead of a deposit slip.

Even then, of course, you run the risk that a lawyer might get you off scot-free.

Danny, an ex-convict who just finished doing five years in prison in Oklahoma, wants to go back. He likes life better behind bars.

"My p.o. (parole officer) wanted me to check into the Topeka state (mental) hospital," Danny told me. "He thinks I'm crazy. I don't think I'm crazy. I just think I understand things, that's all.

"I done five years – you know what I'm saying? – and after that long, you're conditioned. It's your life."

I told Danny I'd somehow gotten the impression that being in prison really isn't that much fun, what with overcrowded conditions, the shady kinds of people you have to fraternize with, etc.

"I get kept in single cells," Danny – not his real name – said.

How so?

"If they put somebody in a cell with me, I stab 'em or threaten to stab 'em, and they put me in a cell alone."

Danny said he'd actually punctured only one guy. In self-defense.

"All you got to do is talk crazy to 'em to get put in lockup."

Lockup?

"Lockup is jail. They got jail inside prison, OK? Most people don't like it. I do. I don't have to get up to go eat. I just get to stay in there alone and they bring my food. I call it room service. And you still get yard privileges if you're in there."

How would he describe what prison's like?

"What's it like? You stand in line, and you get told everything. You get told when to go to chow and when to go to bed. But the main thing is, you don't got to do nothing. And everybody's the same in the joint except the guards."

Danny, who quit school after the sixth grade but got his high school equivalency diploma in prison, says one big reason he prefers prison is that nobody on the outside wants to hire ex-cons for any jobs that pay very well, if they'll hire them at all.

"The parole boys try to play a game with you," he said. "You're supposed to wash dishes for the rest of your life, but

I don't know any ex-cons who can live on less than six bucks an hour. So if you're gonna live, you gotta do crime."

I asked Danny, who was raised in Wichita and lives in the area again now, when it was he first broke a law.

"The first time? Oh, gee. I was 6 or 7. I stole some gum."

Why?

"I wanted the gum."

By the time he was 13, Danny said, he was uncontrollable.

By the time he was 14, he was in Pittsburg Children's Court Center "for burglary and stuff like that."

Burglary is also how he ended up doing the five years he just finished. That, coupled with a charge of possession of a firearm after a previous felony conviction.

I asked Danny, if he had his life to live over, knowing what he knows now, if he'd do anything differently.

"Why, sure. I'd be born a Kennedy or a Rockefeller."

Meanwhile, he just wants to go back to prison without having to commit any risky crimes.

"It'll take me five years to get used to society again," he said.

I wish him luck. Not in getting back into the joint of his choice. But on making it on the outside. And he should take heart. A lot of non-ex-cons don't have it so easy, either.

––––––

Proving to Kids There Are No Monsters

January 12, 1986

Is there anything in life more awful than having nightmares when you're a kid and then having to lie in bed scared out of your wits almost every night?

What's under the bed? In the closet? What are those sounds outside the window? Those strange shadows on the wall? And even if the monsters under your bed don't eat you up, what new nightmares will you dream tonight?

If only there were something convincingly reassuring we could tell our kids to make their fears go away at night.

If only kids would understand that if the evil things they fear actually existed and prowled the planet, there would be proof.

Because if there were anything to these fears that most children share, we would see stories in the newspapers and on TV like these:

Scaly Green Goblin
Devours 11-Year-Old

DERBY – An 11-year-old boy was eaten in his bedroom here Friday night, and Derby police suspect it was the work of the dreaded scaly green graveyard goblin, which is known to prefer fifth-graders.

Werewolves Harass Child

GOODLAND – The Goodland Animal Control Department on Friday confirmed another report of a pack of werewolves leaping out of a closet in a Goodland home and getting hair and fleas all over a child's bed.

Another Youth Turns Into Vampire

JUNCTION CITY – A 9-year-old Junction City girl who forgot to have her parents check under her bed for vampires before turning in for the night was bitten on the neck Friday about 11:15 p.m., and turned into a vampire.

The International Vampire Control Bureau said this was the 1,247,415th vampire bite since 1975, and the girl has been confined with other juvenile Kansas vampires in the

Count Dracula Memorial Home for the Undead in Derby, Kan.

Blob Destroys Dallas

DALLAS – A huge, hairy, jelly-like blob crawled out from under the bed of Danny McBrittle, 10, of 1419 Red Oak Circle in Dallas, Saturday night, and quickly swallowed Danny, his bike, his sister, his parents, his best friend down the street and the rest of the whole city of Dallas.

Gremlins Strike Again; Victim Escapes!

WICHITA – A 13-year-old boy who had been having trouble sleeping nights because he was afraid there were monsters in the hall closet outside his bedroom door survived an alleged attack by five gremlins Friday night.

Police said it was fortunate that the boy had been lying with his eyes alertly open looking for such monsters because when the gremlins charged out of the hall closet to pounce on him, he managed to escape to his parents' bedroom, where his father fought off the fierce beasts with an old Louisville Slugger baseball bat.

In a statement made at City Hall this morning, Police Chief Richard LaMunyon said gremlins now rank as the No. 2 problem in the city behind only ghosts, and he said police efforts to wipe out ghosts, goblins, ghouls and gremlins would be intensified.

Pod From Space Replaces Teenager
With Emotionless Look-Alike

EL DORADO – The invasion of the bodysnatchers continued for the 30th year Saturday when another Earthling youth disappeared and was replaced by a look-alike that is unnaturally calm, emotionless and totally indifferent to all outside stimuli such as rock music, car horns, MTV hairstyles and the ringing of the family telephone.

Police say the 14-year-old girl's parents grew suspicious when they noticed how radically improved her behavior was, and when they looked in their basement they discovered an empty pod.

There. Kids? See? You can relax. Never have there been stories like those anywhere. So sleep tight. And sweet dreams.

You have nothing scarier or more awful to fear than Boy George.

Thoughts I Couldn't Put a Stop to . . .

Ever wish that after reading your newspaper, you could return it for your money back if you didn't like the day's news?

•

Grown women who talk baby talk when they're not talking to babies make me nervous.

•

Ever wonder what Adam and Eve, with no music written yet, hummed and whistled when they were in good moods?

•

Best oxymoron I've heard in a while? Bob Hope Special.

•

Why do so many young comedians yell their monologues? It doesn't help.

Contemplating Fame and the Famous

*"Every time these grown women got together, you
expected a pajama party to break out."*

1977

Under the Influence of James Dean

Watched a movie on TV the other night about a boy and his comb.

"Rebel Without a Cause."

James Dean.

I had to watch it, you see. What I mean is, I hadn't seen it before, so I actually *needed* to see it.

Why? Simple. Because this was the socially semi-significant 1955 flick that helped shape, or bend out of shape, my own esteemed generation, and all these many years I've wondered what I missed.

The reason I didn't see the movie when it came out was that I was a little too young and, after that, I guess I was just never in the right place at the right time to catch it.

I didn't even fully realize until 1962 how much influence James Dean had on some people my age. That was when I went to work on a job where I became friends with the great, shamelessly intense Rick B. Smoothe.

Rick B. Smoothe was living proof that James Dean had not brooded in vain. To him, James Dean wasn't just a crazed movie star. He was a philosophy of life.

As interpreted by Rick B. Smoothe, the James Dean Philosophy of Life was (1) never drive slower than 75 unless you're still in your garage, (2) never drive on a straight road when curves around mountains are available, (3) always look broodingly intense and sullen and never smile unless you strike oil the way Dean did in "Giant," and (4) always make everything you do as dramatic as humanly possible, be it (a) rolling a drunk for a little spending money, (b) leering *preliminarily* at a girl you're planning to overwhelm with charm, or (c) eating a tuna sandwich in the office cafeteria.

So great and profound was James Dean's influence on Rick B. Smoothe that he once confided to me and the other people within range of his voice all over the office: "If my hair was just a little darker and I weren't so tall, I'd look just like James Dean."

Rick B. Smoothe may be the only man who ever lived who was 6-foot-1 or -2 and wished he were 5-foot-7 or -8.

As time went by, I eventually saw "Giant" and "East of Eden," and while James Dean's talent and unique presence as an actor were undeniable, it baffled me how this sometimes almost creepy-acting guy with some basket-case mannerisms had such impact on intelligent young people like Rick B. Smoothe.

I had to conclude that it must have been one incredibly dynamic performance in "Rebel" that did the trick.

So Friday I got a chance to find out. And I'm still baffled.

As infantile '50ish movies go, "Rebel" is pretty unbelievable, makes little sense, and is better than average.

James Dean, who is sincere, moves to this town, see, where Natalie Wood is going steady with a gang of high school punks who like to stick people with knives. Naturally, this little guy – Dean – with his chin on his chest keeps baiting the whole gang until a contest is arranged and, consequently, Natalie's No. 1 boyfriend drives off a cliff and is killed.

Well, Natalie doesn't get over the death of her boyfriend for several minutes, but when she finally does, it occurs to her that even though this new kid in town acts like a basket case, slithering around with his chin on his chest, mumbling and looking out of the tops of his eyes all the time, he's sincere.

Ultimately then, Natalie gets her head together and, with as much feeling as her big eyes can muster (and no doubt speaking for everybody who was a kid between 1950 and 1955), she says to James Dean with a delightfully ironic verb, "Nobody acts sincere."

"Ummmmmrrrrsgghhh," Dean mumbles, presumably trying to agree.

I don't know. I think I'm glad I didn't see "Rebel" when I was in my teens. As impressionable as I've always been, I'm afraid it might have messed up my mind worse than it did Rick B. Smoothe's.

I don't think it would have caused me to spend my entire youth driving stolen cars off cliffs and walking around brooding with my chin on my chest, looking at people from the tops of my eyes.

Worse. I'm afraid it would have caused me to be sincere.

And then where would I have been?

———

Our Kind of Cat, Sinatra Is . . .

October 16, 1981

Any 65-year-old white guy who can get away with going out in public and jauntily walking around snapping his fingers and calling people "cats" has got to be special.

Or senile.

("Oh, my God, Wilma! Grampa is doing it again! How'd he get out of his room this time? We're just going to have to keep a better eye on him, darling, or every time we turn around, he's going to sneak out in public and make a fool of himself snapping his fingers and calling people 'cats'!")

But Frank Sinatra is hardly senile, of course.

He's always been that way.

What way?

You know what way.

His way.

Whatever that means.

Sinatra.

How lucky for Wichita he came to town.

Saves us from having to make a pilgrimage to Vegas to see him sometime.

And he is special, all right.

As overworked and abused as the term may be, Sinatra is, of course and indeed, a genuine living legend. You might even set him apart further by saying he's a living legend's living legend. A god's god. A myth's myth.

And if he comes to town, you go see him.

Not going would be like covering your eyes when Halley's comet is in the neighborhood.

But I won't go quite so far as to say it would be like ignoring the Second Coming.

Even if that's exactly what it was, Sinatra's second time in town.

Sinatra. He's been a living legend so long he must be thinking of moving on to other things. Knighthood? Sainthood?

All my life, I think, Sinatra has been referred to as something of a legend. In my youth, he was at least a budding legend, I imagine.

When he meets new people at parties and bus stops and they ask him, "And what do you do?" he probably says, "Oh, I'm a living legend."

Or he might say, "I used to be a living legend, but then I got too old. I had to take up something less strenuous. It didn't require any heavy lifting, but there was a lot of exertion, all the same. And the hours were awful!"

The man comes to Wichita, you go see him. People who didn't go must have either not started saving up soon enough to buy tickets, or they're the kind of people who would stop at the Louvre just to use the bathroom. Just don't have any idea what they're missing.

Sinatra – he's a living legend, an institution, a myth, a monument, a shrine, the grand poobah of entertainment.

If only he could sing – just kidding, just kidding.

The way Sinatra is, you don't just go to watch him perform, you go to pay homage to him. Or, put another way, it's like you pay 15 or 20 bucks, and Frank grants you an audience. So what if he doesn't sing as well as he used to. Maybe you'll get lucky and he'll let you kiss his ring.

Sinatra. Much to my surprise and delight Tuesday night, Sinatra showed he has a lot of good music left in him to sing for us.

He may have to use mirrors and sleight of hand to handle a few notes, but he is a helluva good show. Now what I can't understand is why his latest single, "New York, New York," is so awful. He sang it much better Tuesday night than on the record. He ought to erase it and do it over.

Ah, but Sinatra is cool. Even if he kept talking on and on about what a super TV show "Gunsmoke" is and about how he wishes it were still on the air, his patter was warm and winning. My favorite line was when he said he knew the Jimmy Razooks (where he was staying east of town) have horses, because he heard the mooing.

Anyway, it was a very good show, Mr. Sinatra.

And now that you know where your wife comes from, don't be such a stranger . . . cat.

Elvis Was Like
a Double Overtime

August 7, 1987

I've been sitting here for numerous minutes now, strenuously thinking as deeply as I can about the seemingly unstoppable Elvis Presley phenomenon.

Giving it all I've got, I have been trying to grasp the cosmic significance, the subtle nuances and the deeper meaning of the man, his music, his lifestyle and his movies, not to mention his peculiar affinity for alarmingly garish jumpsuits and capes.

What can I say? Personally, I liked Elvis' music.

I may not have turned any of the rooms in our house into shrines for Elvis and I may not be completely convinced yet that he was the greatest American who ever lived, but all the same, he sang some terrific songs, and there's no disputing that thanks to Elvis, the world is certainly a more upbeat and entertaining place, especially if you consider all the hilarious Elvis impersonators who have come out from under rocks.

But just how great was Elvis?

Beats me. But I do think some critics have been far too rough on him, so that it's hard to determine sometimes whom they're really taking too seriously – Elvis or themselves.

You know the kind of critics I mean, the ones who scribble such profundities as, "Although Presley, who did not go to Harvard or even Mississippi State, may have been the most popular, dynamic and influential white singer who ever lived, still he was no Caruso, he was no Sinatra, he was no

Neil Armstrong, he was no Olivier, he was no cure for cancer, and when it came to making really ethereal music, he most definitely was no gold-winged Canadian warbler (*vermivora chrysoptera*)."

Yawwwn. Right.

Actually, Elvis Presley influenced my life.

I was about 11 when Elvis came on the scene, but I never really noticed him at first, because music was not very high on my list of priorities. At the time, I thought that the real meaning of life was sports, and the only specific thing that really mattered in the grand scheme of things was how the Cleveland Indians did.

But then came that historic point in American history when word got around that this singer, Elvis Presley, was going to be on the Ed Sullivan Show, and it was causing quite a national commotion, because he jumped around and shook his hips or something.

So I and my best buddy, classmate, and fellow sports fanatic, Burrhead Burns, so named because of his world-class crew cut, decided to check it out.

And we couldn't believe it. Burrhead and I stared at the TV screen, shocked.

Here was this guy with a guitar, and all he was doing was singing and swaying and making faces, yet he was driving all these girls in Ed Sullivan's audience wild! They were shrieking and yelling and wringing their hands, hysterically.

Burrhead watched in awe. He could not believe that a mere singer could work up a bunch of girls into the same kind of frenzy that you ordinarily would never see unless they were in the crowd at an important championship basketball game, and then it would happen only if the game was coming down to an incredibly exciting finish. In fact, this Elvis Presley was affecting those girls like a double overtime.

Why, it looked as if singing rock 'n' roll was a great way to impress girls without even having to win a letter jacket.

Burrhead sat, transfixed, visions of Rita Kay, the dazzling, sexy siren of Mr. Sodervic's sixth-grade class, dancing in his head.

That night, I had no idea how much impact Elvis had on Burrhead. But the very next morning, Burrhead arrived very uncharacteristically early at school, claimed a strategic spot by the sixth-grade door, and when the dazzling Rita Kay arrived, he made his eyelids droopy, curled his upper lip into a horrifying sneer, shook his hips and crooned throatily, "You ain't nothin' but a houn' dog."

I watched, amazed. Because Rita Kay shrieked at Burrhead, just the way all those girls on the Ed Sullivan show had shrieked at Elvis.

And then she bashed him upside the head with her arithmetic book.

_____

Royal Wedding Needed Dwarfs or Mice

July 25, 1986

Before going out to resume painting the house and splattering my face with "stormy petrel" gray on Wednesday evening, I watched some of the royal wedding on TV.

There's no getting around it, this was a pretty impressive royal production, especially if you like large weddings and magnificence.

This was marriage as theater, matrimony as entertain-

45

ment, nuptials as show biz, real life imitating fairy tales.

All this wedding needed was a plot, and you would have sworn it was a Disney production, the sequel maybe to "Snow White" or "Cinderella."

As it was, I found myself searching the TV screen, looking for some sign of talking mice, beaming little dwarfs, fairy godmothers, glass slippers and jabbering mirrors.

But even without them, it was some production. With all the trumpets, horses, carriages, fancy uniforms and general pageantry, it was so spectacular in its British way that it reminded me of the ultimate halftime show at a college football bowl game.

The only thing missing, as extravaganzas go, were some baton twirlers. But then, I didn't see much of the pre-vows procession, so maybe I missed them. I always miss the good stuff.

I didn't miss the actual exchanging of vows, though. And I was so awed that all I could think was, "Gosh, I wish I were the archbishop of Canterbury." What a regal title.

Imagine how it would feel to make a phone call and say, "Hi. This is the archbishop of Canterbury speaking. I'd like a large, deep-pan pepperoni pizza to go, please."

Boy, would people be impressed, even if nobody knows what it means.

Of course, I realize some people are put off by a lot of showy pageantry like that, no matter how tastefully it's done.

For instance, some people don't even appreciate the annual Academy Awards ceremonies, even when Cher is a presenter and wears one of her magnificent gowns that are always so spectacularly flashy they look like they probably require batteries.

And speaking of threads, did you read that the royal bride's gown had a 17 1/2-foot train dragging along behind her?

What can you say to that except there's one woman who really knows how to get married?

With a wedding dress that size, a woman doesn't need bridesmaids to help her get dressed, she needs circus roustabouts to help get the thing on and operative.

Duchess Fergie probably had to spend weeks just practicing walking in all that dress. Imagine if she'd tripped and fallen. It probably would have taken hours to find her under all that material, and by then, she probably would have been smothered.

Covered wagons didn't have that much material on them. In fact, I haven't seen that much cloth on my TV screen since "Wagon Train" went off the air. And I wouldn't have been surprised during the wedding if Ward Bond had turned out to be driving the gown.

But maybe the dress is a lot more practical than it looked. Maybe Prince Andrew, being a flight instructor in the Royal Navy, can use some of it for a parachute.

Fancy weddings like that just aren't my style, though.

I would have been more impressed if Andy had picked up Fergie at her upstairs window by ladder, and they'd climbed down and eloped.

Roy Orbison – Rock's Least Likely Legend

December 9, 1988

I was courageously and absentmindedly attacking my morning beard with my double-edged shaving weapon this morning while wondering about the meaning of life before noon, when Bob Edwards' voice on National Public Radio cut through my personal early morning fog.

Over the sound of running water in the sink, I could hear Edwards say that rock 'n' roll legend Roy Orbison had died of a massive heart attack late last night.

Roy Orbison . . .

Sunglasses and jet-black hair.

Roy Orbison . . .

Running Scared. Only the Lonely. It's Over. Dream Baby. In Dreams. Mean Woman Blues. Cryin'. Blue Bayou. Oh, Pretty Woman.

I put down my razor and turned up the radio.

If I remember right, NPR's Edwards mentioned that Orbison had a history of heart problems and then they played the opening, pounding, dynamic sounds that lead into "Pretty woman, walking down the street, pretty woman, kind I'd like to meet . . . "

And then Bob Edwards moved on from the death of rock 'n' roll legend Orbison to the next important topic of the morning.

Shortly afterward, I left for work. In my car I have two tapes I put together once of some of my favorite songs from various albums.

I have three Orbison songs on the tapes. Driving along, I fast-forwarded until I found the first of them.

"Dowm dowm dowm dowby doo waaah . . . Only the lonely . . . know the heartache that I feel . . . "

Even when I was very young, I had trouble dealing with rock's doo-wahs, wah-ooohs, yay-yay-yays, etc. But when Roy Orbison sang those usually goofy sounds, I not only approved, but, if nobody was around so that I felt sufficiently isolated from the rest of the human race, I'd sometimes even sing along, wah-oooh, wah-oooh.

What can I say? Orbison fans know what I'm talking about. Roy Orbison made music that was almost impossible to resist wailing along with, even if you had a voice like a smoke alarm.

Over the entire day at work, I saw that only two stories about the legendary Roy Orbison came over the wires, both of them your standard obituaries rather than a special tribute you'd expect your basic legends to get.

"Roy Orbison, whose personal life mirrored the tragic themes of his music, died Tuesday night in a Hendersonville, Tenn., hospital.

"The singer and composer, who had transcended mere performing to become a legend of the country-oriented component of rock 'n' roll that he had pioneered, was 52."

The more I've thought about Roy Orbison always being called a legend, the more impressive it seems.

Think of it. That Orbison became a music legend is really amazing.

That is, all the man really had going for him was his voice.

He was an unimpressive-looking man. His stage presence was close to comatose. And yet he "transcended mere performing to become a legend."

He didn't do it with charisma beyond that of his voice. Not by wearing weird clothes. Not by shake, rattle and rolling. Not by pumping iron. Not by punching writers, smashing guitars, dying his hair green nor by making movies featuring lots of lovely young ladies serving as co-stars and scenery.

Nope. Roy Orbison became a legend the hard way. By having the talent to turn out 27 straight hit records. Amazing, isn't it?

But let me tell you how much I really liked Orbison's music back in the days when he had so many hits that it was as though he were providing half the background music for part of my youth.

Back in those days, when I was in my early 20s, I made so little money that I very rarely splurged on record albums. And when I did decide I liked somebody's music enough to buy a whole album's worth of his songs, it was a major event for me.

And I had so few albums then that I can remember most of them:

There was Elvis' Golden Hits. The "West Side Story" sound track. Johnny Mathis. Andy Williams. One by the Lettermen, with the incomparable "The Way You Look Tonight." Rick Nelson. The great Dion. And two Roy Orbisons.

That might not mean anything to you.

But it sort of explains why I felt really lousy off and on Wednesday.

Mercy.

———

Is Michael Jackson's Success, Well, Weird?

June 27, 1984

Next!

Bring on the next strange rock superstar, please.

I've had it up to here with Michael Jackson.

It's nothing personal. I dislike most rock stars anymore. But the others you can ignore. You just close your eyes to MTV when you're changing channels and bash in your car radio with an ax.

But Michael Jackson you can't ignore. He's everywhere.

Everywhere you go, everywhere you look, everywhere you listen, there he is, cute little curl twisting down his forehead, shades over his eyes real cool-like. Singing. Dancing. Selling Pepsi.

Forgive me, modern youth, but I don't understand the Michael Jackson phenomenon.

If he were moderately successful, I'd understand that. After all, he's some dancer, and his music is catchy.

But this guy hasn't merely made the world forget Elton John, why, he's the hottest thing since the Beatles!

Amazing.

Don't get me wrong, youthful persons. I do not remain unthrilled by Michael Jackson because I myself am not a youth anymore.

I remain unthrilled by Michael Jackson because of the kind of person I am – nasty, but courageous with terrific taste and judgment.

Even as a youth, I had very good taste and judgment when it came to pop music. You don't have to get old to dislike bad music.

When I was kid, if a song had more than two '"doo wops" or more than one "lamma lamma ding dong,"I scoffed.

Fortunately, of course, there were a lot of great singers back then. Danny and the Juniors. Little Richard. The Monkees. Fabian. All the immortal Bobbys. Shelley Fabares. Frankie Avalon. The incomparable Dion.

"Ohhh, I'm the kyna guyuy whooo liiikes to roammmm arroun, where pretty girls are, welll that's where I'll be foun'!"

Ah, what a golden age of music that was.

Know where I'd rank Michael Jackson among the all-time rock giants?

Clear up there with Chubby Checker.

Chubby gave us the Twist. Michael introduced the Moonwalk.

Next!

Most likely, Michael Jackson's massive success is probably caused by modern youth's need for singers to scream at.

After the thrill of Bee Gees (who sounded like Alvin and the Chipmunks – or, at best, Frankie Valli and the Chipmunks) and KISS wore off for America's youth, Jackson probably was just in the right place at the right time. So he was the next singer youth chose to scream at.

Screaming at singers goes way back, of course. According to ancient history, screaming and shouting were invented by some promoters who were hustling a product called Frank Sinatra. They planted some girls in the audience who screamed and fainted, and the rest is history.

In time, youth screamed at Elvis, at George, Paul, John and Ringo, and after that, at anybody with a guitar.

Youth even screamed at the Dave Clark Five. That shows you how desperate youth is to scream at singers.

Do you realize, modern youth, that there are middle-aged women right now – maybe your neighbor, maybe your teacher or maybe even your very own mother – who screamed at the Dave Clark Five?

No doubt they'll never admit it now. But that's probably where you inherited your silliness.

And that's probably why, when Michael Jackson dynamically points his index fingers, you feel so electrified you. . . .

Screeeeaaaammmmmmmm!

Ah, well, youth. In time, you'll get over your impulses that make you want to spend $30 for tickets to behave pseudo-hysterically over Michael Jackson.

In time, you'll mature and start behaving like an adult.

In other words, in time, you'll spend your $30 for a couple of soccer tickets to go out to the Kansas Coliseum, shout profanities at St. Louis players, dump beer on the bums' heads and, well, screeeeaaaammmmmmm.

Beware of Ozzy – He Bites (Bats)

March 9, 1986

An unusual person called Ozzy Osbourne who bites bats is coming to Wichita soon to perform at the Kansas Coliseum.

I'm very excited and looking forward to this occasion and hope I will be able to attend so I can see him bite a bat.

This Ozzy person is multitalented, too. He doesn't just bite bats for a living. He also makes noise with electrical machinery such as guitars and other electrical tools and amplifying appliances.

This sort of noise is called, appropriately, heavy metal, which means noise played loud enough so that people sitting in the back row have no trouble hearing – even if they're in the back row on another continent.

This is not the sort of easy-listening music said to soothe the savage breast.

This is music to have a nervous breakdown by. Music to set off dynamite by. Music to get you in the mood for World War III. Music to bite bats by.

Actually, Ozzy O. doesn't merely bite bats.

He bites the suckers' little heads right off.

I can't think of the last time I was so impressed by a musician's act. And are you thinking what I'm thinking?

This Ozzy fellow could be the answer to our prayers, the solution to Wichita's horrifying crow problem.

Here's my thinking. We hire Ozzy and his noisemaking accomplices to scare off the crows. We send Odd Ozzy and his buddies out into the streets to stun the crows with their loud noises, nab them, bite their heads off and toss them in Hefty bags.

Imagine the results. The remaining crows would be so terrified that they would hop the very first bus out of town and probably not stop going until they got to some place really far away such as Sydney, Australia, or Neptune.

I'd love to meet Mr. Osbourne to discuss this. And I might even like him, because he reminds me of another creature I was once fond of.

Years ago when my grandparents were alive, living on their farm, they had a dog that was a lot like Ozzy Osbourne, except Rover didn't play an electrified guitar. Instead, he howled at the moon, farm lights, airplanes, the sun and just about anything else that either gave off light or moved. I imagine he and Ozzy would have had a lot in common.

As you might guess, Rover was actually an exceptionally warm, friendly mutt when it came to people, especially little kids. But as for anything else, he tended to make a determined effort to bite their heads off. Birds. Chickens. Ducks. Cats. Squirrels. Cows.

Odd Ozzy even looks a little like Rover, except Rover had less hair and was cuter.

Speaking of hair, I found a picture of Ozzy taken a couple of years ago when he shaved his head, apparently causing, as suggested by the photo, his head to tilt precariously and his eyes to bulge.

Of course, Odd Oz had a very good reason to shave his head, even though he wasn't becoming a professional wrestler.

The story said he had put too much dye in his hair. And, like any of the rest of us do when we put too much purple, green or orange dye in our hair so that it takes on the texture of a dried, matted, used paintbrush that was not cleaned and sat in the garage 14 months, Ozzy solved his strange personal problem by whacking it all off.

But even if Odd Ozzy isn't interested in chasing our crows away, I still can't wait to see him. I just hope he talks, too.

That's because extraordinary human-like creatures like Ozzy usually make terrific columns.

For instance, I have interviewed Turtle Girl, Susie the Snake Woman, Minnie the Mermaid, Renaldo the Sword-Swallower, Lobster Man and even God himself, who, in case you missed the column a few years ago, is a rather timid, misunderstood being who lives in Ohio and even sent me a book which I still mean to read someday.

I have only two questions about Ozzy Osbourne's performance.

How much will people be paid to go out and gawk at him in hopes he'll bite a bat's head off?

And is he, like Rover ended up, kept on a heavy, short chain?

———

But Does Springsteen Help Move Pianos?

December 10, 1986

My turn to write about Bruce Springsteen.

I mean, why should I be the only person left on this planet who has the alphabet at his disposal who has not yet written about Bruce Springsteen and his hot, new $25 five-record retrospective?

And, incidentally, the local record stores tell me the set continues to sell pretty well, thank you, but there are still plenty to go around just in case you're stuck for gift ideas and would like to buy 15 or 20 to give to friends or people you might pass on the street who look needy.

Now. I'm really curious about one thing.

I thought if you were a singer, you were supposed to be either dead, a has-been, a yodeler or a religious warbler before they brought out these multi-record sets like this, and even then, don't they usually only hawk these special marathon music ordeals as late-night TV offers? Something like so:

"Hurry, hurry, everyone, get out your checkbook or grab your credit card, here it is, yessiree, your big chance, a once-in-a-lifetime opportunity for you to own almost every single solitary song Bruce Screamsteen ever sung, every note he ever hummed, strummed, plunked or shrieked, every tune he ever sweated out of his system, every word he ever struggled to enunciate, including all those records you never had any desire to buy back before Bruce had biceps!

"Included in this special offer are all his mega-hits with catchy, powerful short titles! 'Sweating'! 'Aching'! 'Tired'! 'Restless'! 'Anxious'! 'Morose'! And 'Feverish'!

"Yes, music lovers and rock fans, you can have all these big hits plus many, many more, all for just $24.99, album or cassette, or just $44.99 for compact discs!

"Also included in this incredible set are Bruce's clever send-ups of other singers' superior songs! 'I Left My Heart in Honest John's Used Car Lot'! 'Spaghetti and Meatballs for a Blue Lady'! 'I'll Save the Last Greasy French Fry for You'! And 'Just Singing in the Car Wash'!

"And that's not all! Then there are these classics, too! 'I Gave My Baby a Genuine Denim Jacket'! 'Never Trust Nobody Who Doesn't Have Grease Under Their Fingernails'! 'Alice's Calluses'! 'Please Stop Sticking Your Bubblegum Up Under My Motorcycle Seat, Bertha'! 'She

56

Isn't Just Another Pretty Face, She's Got Some Great Tattoos, Too'! And then there is Bruce's greatest hit, 'Would You Still Love Me if I Shaved and Bathed?'

"Yes! You can have this great record set for only $24.99, and if you act now, we'll include a bonus poster of Bruce sweating!"

Personally, I like Bruce Springsteen better than any of the other rock stars who have come along in years, because he strikes me as the sort of regular guy who would be happy to come over to your place and help you move your piano. I'll bet he might even be the sort of good guy who offers to jump-start his friends' cars even when they don't need it.

Springsteen has always reminded me of Al Pacino playing a rock star who hopes he'll get a decent enough gig someday so he can buy some socially acceptable clothes, otherwise he's about ready to chuck it all and go back to work at his brother's filling station.

What a wardrobe this guy has. His designer must be a pit bull. His shirt sleeves are ripped off! He's got holes in his jeans! He looks like he wears the Hell's Angels' hand-me-downs.

To become more of an authority on his actual music and to hear what he sounds like, I listened to a whole Springsteen tape the other night.

But I'm reserving judgment. I don't think that was a representative album I heard, the kind that made him a superstar. No tape like that could catapult a guy to cult status.

I mean, on this album, he sounded awfully hoarse and raspy, like he had a horribly sore throat when he recorded it. And as a result, I guess, most of the songs even sounded monotonously alike.

The tape was "Born in the U.S.A."

Probably never did anything. Ever heard of it?

Talk About "Strange,"
Talk About "Crazy"

June 22, 1986

I always had a gnawing feeling that being open-minded would be my ruin someday.

Look what's happened.

I bought a country music record album last week.

"Patsy Cline's Greatest Hits."

I don't know what this means.

Maybe it's just another strange musical phase I'm going through.

But maybe, more alarmingly, it is the first danger sign that I might be turning into a country music fan. Or, almost as bad, maybe I have built up some kind of tolerance for listening to country tunes.

All I know is I had to buy this record.

Something beyond my control and understanding has happened to me. It's like I had a major spiritual experience – that you can slow-dance to.

"I . . . faaaall . . . toooo . . . piecesssssssss. . . . "

It all happened so fast, getting hooked on Patsy Cline.

About a week ago, I rented a VCR and my family open-mindedly watched "Sweet Dreams," the movie about Patsy Cline's short life.

The woman's voice knocked me out. That's all there is to it.

This was about the greatest "music to cry in your beer by" that I had ever heard.

Occasionally, a single song by somebody will get to me like that. But not song after song by the same person.

58

I might prefer Streisand's kinds of songs as a rule, and Streisand might have a more spectacular, showy voice. But this Miss Patsy Cline went places with her voice and her songs that I don't think Barbra Streisand will ever even know about, let alone go.

Heck, Patsy Cline could get more emotion and feeling and mileage out of the word "dreams" than most singers can wring out of their whole careers.

I'm sorry. Excuse my disgusting enthusiasm. But you know how we fanatics are. Especially us brand-new ones.

But it wasn't just me. My whole family was taken by her singing, and my two girls usually don't like any music unless it sounds like it's being sung by somebody with purple hair who is making disgusting facial expressions and acting like they left their minds back home on Neptune.

So what could I do? I had to buy a Patsy Cline record myself to find out whether this woman who died in a plane crash at the age of 30 really sounded as extraordinary on regular records as she did in the movie (in which Jessica Lange did an Academy Award-caliber job of lip-synching, not to mention all-around acting).

The record sounded just as good as the movie.

Side Two is so-so. Side One is magic: "Walking After Midnight." "Sweet Dreams." "Crazy." "I Fall to Pieces." "Strange." And my favorite, the steamily sultry "So Wrong."

My wife likes the record, too, but she can't believe my overreaction. Now she keeps expecting me to buy a pickup truck with a gun rack. Or maybe bring a freight train home for dinner.

But all I want to know is why Patsy Cline wasn't hailed as about the world's greatest singer person while she was alive. Was it because she was country and country wasn't cool yet? Her songs aren't that country. She didn't have fiddles. She didn't howl and wail and whine. Maybe if she just hadn't died so young. . . .

You listen to this wonderful voice performing its dazzling little miracles with words and emotions, and you think, hey, forget the philosophers and the preachers and the teachers, boys and girls, here is a human who must know all there is to know about joy and sorrow and love and life and longneck beer bottles and dusty country roads, and, best of all, she doesn't express herself through her nose.

Maybe I'm overreacting. Maybe I've been working too hard. Or maybe I'm kidding myself and I'm actually infatuated with Jessica Lange.

I just don't know. It's like one of those wailing country philosophers once wondered:

What in the world's come over me?

———

10 Reasons Kansans Endure David Letterman

October 30, 1989

Maybe you heard. Some nut in New York has been harassing Kansans by telephone.

Maybe you're way ahead of me and had your phone number changed and unlisted or, to be safer still, moved to a less threatened state. I wouldn't blame you.

What's this world coming to, I want to know, when a Wichitan hesitates to answer the phone out of fear there may be some comedian calling to make unfunny jokes?

This particular nut is a white male, probably about 6 feet tall, medium build, with curiously swirling brown hair.

He has two special, distinguishing characteristics – a

dangerously endearing gap between his two upper front teeth, a la venerable model and professional character Lauren Hutton, and sneakers that one suspects can be removed only surgically.

David Letterman is the crackpot's name.

He has this late-night TV show, which some people actually watch.

It's an intentionally offbeat, off-the-wall show that is probably stranger than it thinks it is or means to be.

In lieu of being amusing very much, Letterman simply projects an attitude, and that always seems to make the strange audiences laugh bafflingly at anything he says, no matter how unfunny.

Naturally, I've watched the Letterman show, once all the way through.

That was the night I forced myself to stay awake late to watch Gene Scott, the wacky TV evangelist who used to be on the air after Letterman and who was infinitely funnier.

Anyway, Letterman has taken to calling Kansans, it seems.

Lately, he, while on the air, has been phoning Maurice and Darline Shank of Wichita and making some bets with them on the World Series.

At least once before, I recall, he phoned another Kansan.

The explanation given for these calls to Kansas is that he happens to have a Wichita phone directory, which, I guess, could mean the show might soon have a regular new feature called Dial-a-Kansan.

Whatever. Using Letterman's own comedy tactics, here's my tribute to him for all the attention he's been giving Kansas lately. . . .

The Top 10 Reasons Kansans Say They Watch David Letterman

10. You've already seen "A Place in the Sun" on late-

night TV 505 times and were ready for a change.

9. You're a barber, beautician or dead French emperor, and you just love to sit there and watch his hairstyle.

8. Because he's almost as hip and clever as your talented Uncle Zeke, who makes terrific flatulent sounds with the palms of his hands.

7. You figure anybody who looks like both Ted Koppel and Mad magazine symbol Alfred E. Neuman ought to be paid close attention to.

6. You missed Cher that time she was on the show with Sonny and wore that incredibly skimpy outfit, and you want to make sure you don't miss her the next time she shows up.

5. You think he's so good he's almost in Pat Sajak's league.

4. It's your way of paying penance for some very serious sin or act of stupidity you once committed.

3. By 11:30, when his show comes on, you are so sloshed or stoned you don't even know which network you're watching, and when it happens to be ABC, you even laugh uproariously at Ted Koppel and Sam Donaldson.

2. You want to be sure you're watching the night Letterman does one of those patronizing, obnoxious, on-the-street bits, and some proud, dignified little shopkeeper, who isn't intimidated by the TV cameras, punches his lights out.

1. It keeps you going each year between those wonderfully entertaining Jerry Lewis telethons.

But Was Gomez Addams "30something"?

So they've axed "thirtysomething," huh? The great but grating TV show about all those tiresomely intelligent, oppressively sensitive, relentlessly annoying yuppie persons with all their maddening, exasperating, endless, bottomless *feelings?*

That's too bad.

I hated that show.

I hated that show so much I almost always watched it.

I don't really understand the strange hold it had on me.

There was only one character on the show that I found really likable – Michael Steadman. But even he didn't deserve to be liked, simply because he was married to the hopelessly soulful Hope, who always looked as if she were on the verge of either writing a bad poem, burning her bra or letting you die in her arms.

No matter what happened, good or bad, Hope always looked like this boundlessly well-meaning but sad and long-suffering wife. Which always made you wonder what her problem was, then, since her hubby made the big bucks and her only problem in the world should have been how to get rid of all of her tedious friends.

Strange, strange people.

The supporting characters behind Michael – Hope, Elliott and Nancy – really made the show for me, though.

They were worse.

Week after week, they virtually wallowed in their thirtysomethingness and angst.

63

Having high ideals and big dreams seemed to weigh incredibly heavily on them all.

Gary was so soulful and nice you only wish he'd been killed off in the opening episode years ago.

Gary was this thoroughly idealistic, poetic guy who rode a bicycle and dressed and carried himself in such a way that he seemed to be trying to tell the world that the average deep feeling is more important than, say, buying a good TV or bowling a 200 game. Pathetic.

The four women were worse. They acted like their idea of a fun date would've been group therapy.

They were also *preciously* tight with one another. Every time these grown women got together, you expected a pajama party to break out.

But for all the frequent outbursts of girlishness and boyishness, the show was almost relentlessly heavy and grim.

It desperately needed an occasional injection of lightness, just for a change of pace.

To breathe some welcome, refreshing fun into the show and probably boost the ratings nicely, what I think the show's writers should have done was stick in an occasional upbeat story every three or four weeks.

Imagine a plot in which Hope hired the reunited Charlie's Angels to look for their lost dog.

Imagine Michael, Hope, Nancy and Elliott all taking a cruise on the Love Boat, during which, much to their surprise, Capt. Stubing works out all their problems for them before they get back.

Imagine Elliott, in an exciting case of mistaken identity, involved in a high-speed car chase with Starsky and Hutch.

Imagine the high jinks when who should move in next door to the Steadmans but the eerie yet wonderfully warm and lovable Addams Family.

Or imagine Michael persuading his cold, demonic boss,

Miles, to seek counseling, so Miles starts seeing Dr. Bob (Bob Newhart) Hartley, who would have either completely deflated the puffed-up Miles or sicced his other wacko patients on the poor guy.

Ah, I hate to see "thirtysomething" go. But I hear they might make a few more shows to tie up some loose ends.

That would be great. And I know what they could do.

Because Michael deserves better and ought to get a chance to escape from all his soggy, painfully suffocating friends, the writers could come up with a nice plot to give him a chance to tear free, start over and find happiness.

I wonder if Sam could use another bartender in "Cheers"?

———

Come On, Deeb! Stomp Farrah's Head, Man!

August 8, 1980

Gary Deeb, the sappy, jawless, mushy-eyed, wimpy, chicken-faced, perhaps even twisted twerp whose syndicated TV columns regularly grace the pages of this newspaper, is my hero.

One reason Deeb – I think of him fondly, admiringly as The Incredible Schnook – is my hero is because he's obviously the kind of wonderfully warped guy who would love the way this column is beginning.

But what I admire most about this splendidly crude, rude, maybe even magnificently maladjusted nerd is his salary.

Then after that, what I admire most about Deeb is his apparent lack of any feeling whatsoever for some of his poor subjects.

I mean, when you read Deeb, you kind of feel like one of those maniacal Monday Night wrestling fans or something – *Get 'em, Gare! Atta babe, really stick it to 'em! Gouge his eyes, man! Crush 'im! Come on, Deeb, stomp on Farrah's head for havin' the nerve to be only an adequate actress! Crucify Robert Blake! Mangle the bum! Stomp his head since you don't dig the cat much, man! Make him bleed! Yaaaaayyy!*

They say Deeb makes something like 120 grand now that he has changed desks, shifting from the Tribune to the Sun-Times in Chicago.

According to some people's calculations, that means Deeb is paid $60,000 for each adjective he knows.

Snappy. Which means good.

Sappy. Which doesn't.

But that's incorrect and unfair. Because there is something excitingly primitive about Deeb's style. *Grunt once if you like the show, Gary-baby, twice if you don't.*

Maybe you think I'm just jealous of all the money Deeb makes. Of course I am. Nobody pays me money to watch TV.

Another thing I admire about this great American cheap-shot artist is that he can be so nasty that he makes you feel sorry for performers you don't like any better than he does.

Take Robert Blake. Deeb has called Blake "the psychologically warped actor" and "the loud-mouthed, emotionally troubled actor who starred so stridently in 'Baretta' for four seasons." Deeb wrote that Blake "will star in ... 'Of Mice and Men.' (Incidentally, Blake won't portray the feeble-minded character, which is certainly casting against type.)"

Casually, almost, Deeb tosses "loud-mouthed" out while mentioning Jack Klugman, simply in passing.

Deeb wrote that Shaun Cassidy is a "slack-jawed wimp." Now no matter how little you might think of Shaun

Cassidy, that penetrating observation by Deeb seems so unnecessary and so unprofessional that you want to punch Deeb out yourself.

In one column recently, Deeb called Barry Goldwater an "aging foghorn," Nancy Reagan "cold-blooded" and Pat Boone, Donnie and Marie all "twerps."

Nice guy, this Deeb, huh? In a magazine article not too long ago, Deeb said that he was the "nastiest," "baddest" boy in the neighborhood when he was a kid, "liable to do almost anything – throw a rock through a window, steal candy bars from a drugstore, throw mud on somebody's porch."

Care to jump all over that, amateur psychologists? Help yourselves.

Just keep in mind that Gary Deeb, the aging brat, is one of the best critics in the country. In fact, the abrasive bozo would probably still be just as good and just as readable and even more credible (I mean, who can ever really trust somebody with blood dripping from his fangs?) if he cut out all the unnecessary invective, pointless put-downs and seemingly forced nastiness.

That's what worries me. If the twerp ever grows up and stops slinging mud, I'd be stuck without a hero.

Maybe, just in case, I ought to check out Jack Tatum, the allegedly dirty football player.

What's One More Disgusting, Twisted, Offensive Movie?

August 15, 1988

How about all that high-voltage furor over Martin Scorsese's new flick, "The Last Temptation of Christ"?

I don't know about you but, personally, I really have a hard time taking any biblical movie the least bit seriously if it isn't at least 4 1/2 hours long and doesn't have Charlton Heston in it.

But even so, I've been following the hype and anti-hype about the movie, and after listening to most of Scorsese's interview with Ted Koppel on "Nightline" and seeing some film clips, I really don't know what to say except: What's the big deal about Hollywood coming out with one more movie that a lot of people find disgusting, twisted, spiritually offensive and in the worst possible taste?

What I wonder is how this movie was conceived. Can you imagine the sort of conversations Martin Scorsese might have had in the beginning, going door-to-door, trying to get the project bankrolled?

"But I can make this an artistic and commercial success, J.B.!"

"Forget it, Marty baby, forget it! Religious movies are losers. Nobody wants to see biblical epics anymore."

"But I could make this different, J.B.! I could make it work!"

"Ha! Different? Forget different. I'll tell you a religious epic you could make that would be boffo box office, Marty sweetheart! Make a film about the PTL Club and Jessica Hahn and Jimmy Swaggart! You get the film rights to those stories and I'm with you all the way! I can see it now! Jack Nicholson as Jim Bakker! Dolly Parton as Tammy Faye! Jessica Hahn, making her movie debut, as herself! And Sylvester Stallone as Jimmy Swaggart! What do say, Mart?"

"No, J.B. I've been wanting to do this story for years. Let Spielberg or DePalma do that one."

"Well, Marty, tell me what you'd do to protect my investment? To guarantee me a little profit?"

"For starters, J.B., I'm thinking about modernizing the dialogue. Updating it. Taking out all the 'thees' and 'thous' and stuff like that."

"Not enough, Marty."

"Well, what if I took out all the 'beholdests' and 'begats' and 'yea, verilys,' too?"

"That'd be a start, son. But these are the '80s! It'll take a lot more than that to get people to watch a biblical movie. What if you made the film a little more upbeat and hip? Maybe you could have Jesus deliver the Sermon on the Mount as a rap song?"

"I don't think I'd go quite that far, J.B. But I'd modernize it the best I could. Take the beatitudes. They might go something like this: 'Hey, blessed are the meek, y'know, 'cause they are gonna, like, inherit the whole swinging Earth!'"

"Interesting, Marty."

"So what do you say, J.B.? Are you with me?"

"Well, Martin. You do know, of course, that it's kind of *de rigueurish* these days to work a little sex scene into movies, right? I mean, if word got out there wasn't some, well, spice, in this movie, it'd be box office poison, you know what I mean?"

"Funny you should mention that, J.B. The book my movie is based on has Jesus hallucinating about that very thing. Maybe I could do something with that."

"What, are you kidding me? I'm no biblical scholar, but I just don't remember that from my Sunday school days. But now we're talking! So why don't you just skip all that depressing biblical stuff about lame people and hungry people and crucifixions and just do the whole movie based on the hallucination, Marty?"

"I need to stick to the Bible story, J.B."

"Well, just out of curiosity, what book of the Bible is this hallucination in, anyway?"

"That part isn't exactly in the Bible, J.B."

"No? You mean you're gonna add some major creative details to the Bible, Marty? So now it's like we'll have the Gospel according to Matthew, Mark, Luke, John and Martin? I love it! Now if you can get the right star for the lead, maybe we can talk. How about Burt Reynolds?"

"I don't think so, J.B."

"Tom Selleck? Everybody likes Tom Selleck."

"Wrong image again, J.B."

"Bruce Willis? Tom Cruise? Dennis Quaid?"

Get the, uh, picture, readers?

The movie could have been a lot, lot worse.

———

But Pity John Irving's Weak-Stomached Readers

October 24, 1982
If you loved John Irving's best seller "The Hotel New Hampshire," you should also love . . .
The Motel New Mexico (condensed)
by Irving John

Once upon a time I had a big family. There were Grandpa, Grandma, Papa, Mama, my brothers and sisters, Tom, Phil, Will, Jill, Mavis, Travis, Louis, Lulu, Janie, Ralph and me, Irv.

Grandpa was a retired pro wrestler. Papa was a graduate of Harvard and a dreamer. Grandma and Mama were just women.

Tom was weird. Phil was a creep. Will was 8-foot-1. Jill was a dwarf who wouldn't admit it. Mavis liked opera. Travis and Louis were inseparable. They were also Siamese twins, joined at the ears. Lulu pretended to be deaf by never hearing sounds. Ralph liked to torture insects and Phil. Janie was the most magnificent creature ever to grace this earth – gorgeous, charming and irresistibly vulgar. And I'm Irv. I do 15,000 sit-ups, 5,000 push-ups, run 115 miles and eat 11 dozen bananas every day. What else is there to do?

My family liked pets. We had a dog named Self-Pity, a chicken named Gloom, a cat named Agony, a canary named Despair, a rabbit named Symbolic, a monkey named Pain, and an elephant named Cuddles.

Self-Pity was a gross dog. He stunk something awful, too. But Janie and Papa loved Self-Pity, and Janie always defended it, saying, "@#$%¢&! #$¢&*! @#*& !" But then, Janie *always* said, "@#$%¢&! #$¢&*! @#*& !" about everything.

Because Self-Pity stunk, whenever any of us would mope or feel sorry for ourselves about anything, we started saying, "Self-Pity stinks," and it helped us cope, and sometimes made us giggle philosophically.

One day we found poor little Mavis mauled to death with funny little footprints and "gnaw" marks all over her.

Mama was upset. She asked, "Who did it? And *why?*"

"I think it was Symbolic," said Lulu, meaning our rabbit. And from that moment on, whenever anybody was mauled to death by a rabbit, we would say, "I think it was symbolic." We were so adorable, my family. But we took Mavis' death hard. We didn't get it over it for days.

Papa, the dreamer, had a thing for motels. He liked to buy old buildings with the money Mama inherited after Grandpa got stepped on by Cuddles the elephant, and convert them into motels.

Once, Papa bought Ohio State University just to turn the Fine Arts building into a motel. Papa was really cute that way.

That was the year Janie jilted the Cincinnati Bengals, Lulu was blinded when the oven exploded, Ralph lost an arm in the electric pencil sharpener, Cuddles the elephant lost a leg when she hit a train, and I got a bad toothache.

One sunny day, a motorcycle gang came by the motel and asked Will if he wanted to come out and play. So much for Will. Being such a close family, we really missed him for a while, too.

And from then on, any time a foolish opportunity presented itself, we'd always say, "Never go out and play with a motorcycle gang."

After that motel folded in 1968, Papa decided to move to Saigon and convert an old pagoda into a motel.

We flew over in two planes, so we all wouldn't die if one plane crashed. We were very lucky. Only the plane carrying Mama and Jill crashed. The rest of us arrived safely, but we still felt awful.

Papa named the pagoda the Motel New Mexico, because it sounded good, and our family grew much closer together in war-torn Vietnam, although my sister Janie stubbornly refused to marry me.

One day we went for a ride, set off a land mine, were hit by mortar, took some sniper fire, and had a flat tire. Tom, Travis and Louis were killed. Lulu was horribly disfigured.

Cuddles the elephant lost an ear. But Papa was only blinded by shrapnel.

After that experience, we were all down in the dumps.

"Self-Pity stinks," I reminded everybody. Then we sighed and, finally, giggled philosophically.

Though blinded, Papa didn't want a seeing-eye dog. He said it would remind him of Self-Pity, which had been killed by a maniac with an ax. So we gave Papa a seeing-eye python. He loved it, probably because it was so slimy.

Four years later, we decided to go back to America. Our flight was pretty successful. We came within a couple miles of the coast before we crashed.

I was the only survivor. Losing my whole family and the pets, too, really bothered me, but then I thought, "Wait a minute, Irv. At least you have your many wonderful, disgusting, depraved, revolting, unbelievable memories. Why, I'll bet if you wrote a book about it, I'd make a mint."

Besides, Self-Pity stinks.

———

"Just Call Me Jim, Jessica . . ."

June 7, 1987

Do you think anybody just might have said any of the following?

• "What? You've been offered a job turning letters on a *game show*? Forget it, Vanna honey. Think of your career! Your future!"

• "Michael Jackson! Would you please *forget ab*out having any cosmetic surgery? Leave your face alone! If you want to turn into somebody else so bad, why don't you just

73

change your name?"

• "Listen to me, Koppel. You take that anchor job on the Iran hostage crisis and your career will be over. Kaput! The ratings will be *zero*, Carson will shoot you out of the water, and you'll be lucky if you ever get your ugly mug in front of the camera again!"

• "Say, Sen. Hart! I have a great idea to stop these rumors about you being a womanizer. *Dare* the media to follow you around!"

• "Tone down, Joanie baby. Since you're starting your own talk show and have to last over the long haul, the time has come for Joan Rivers to cut out the nastiness, gush all over everybody, and clap your hands like a deranged seal. Got that? People will love it."

• "Al, dear? It's ABC's 'Nightline!' They say they want you, Al Campanis, on the show to talk about Jackie Robinson! Ohhh, this is so exciting, darling! After all the years you've spent behind the baseball scenes! Why don't we give our tickets to the charity mud wrestling matches to the Lasordas so you can be on national TV? You'll be wonderful! OK?"

• "Go ahead and order the air-conditioned doghouse, Tammy Faye. There's no way our partners would ever find out about it. I mean, you're not planning on inviting any of *them* over, are you, ha ha?"

• "And after this is all over, Lt. Col. North, I imagine you'll be a full colonel before you know it and a general in no time flat! It might be about time to have a military man in the White House. Especially if the right people owe you."

• "Hold a weeklong River Festival? Here in Wichita? Are you kidding! It'd never work. The only way you can draw a crowd in Wichita as large as 45 people is to have a garage sale – on the east side!"

• "Cosby, you're crazy! A family show? What we need

to do is team you up again with Robert Culp. Do another spy show. People don't want warmth! They want action! More 007 stuff! That's the formula for the '80s!"

• "No, no, don't call me *Mr*. Bakker! Just call me *Jim*, Jessica. I'd like to be your friend."

• "Look, Spielberg. I like your idea of a movie about a creature from outer space. But for Pete's sake, man, this sketch you drew is ridiculous! It's so *ugly*, it'll never go over! Why don't you make it look more like, say, a Smurf?"

• "What? *What*? You went ahead with it? You mean you didn't realize we were joking about putting the Kansas Coliseum way out there? Oh, no!"

• "*Pizza*? You want to start a pizza store, boys? Frank? You're the sensible one. Talk some sense into your brother Dan. Running a little restaurant is nice, fellas, but how you gonna make enough money to support a family?"

• "Considering the energy crisis, you know what we here at KG&E could do that would not only be farsighted but would *really* enhance our image with the public? We could put up a nuclear power plant!"

• "Marcia? I'm afraid the attorney general has decided to let you go. No hard feelings, OK?"

• "Getz? Welcome to the newspaper business, boy. But let me tell you one thing before you start a career. Journalism isn't all glamour."

Is Kitty Kelley Ruining Fame?

April 29, 1991

It's sinful. A crime. Really irritating. Biographers today are taking all the fun out of becoming rich, famous and powerful.

It's sad, not to mention very disillusioning.

Who's even going to want to be rich, famous and powerful anymore, the way some biographers treat you?

It's like the Bible says:

What shall it profit a man to gain the whole world, even including membership in the ritziest country clubs, if Kitty Kelley is just going to come along and ravage your reputation with a nasty, unauthorized, excessively truthful, rumoroozing biography?

So why bother succeeding at anything, anymore, when the risk is just too great that if you do, you'll end up the victim of some viciously avaricious, disreputably gifted writer who's looking for a nice, fresh, juicy reputation to sink his or her typewriter into.

Take me. I'd be scared to death to get rich and famous.

I'd be picked to pieces.

You know how it works.

My ex-wife would write a book about what a defective husband I was.

My son would write a book about what a defective father I was.

My sister would write a book about what a defective brother I was.

My aunts and uncles would write a book no doubt portraying me as the world's most defective living nephew.

My ex-neighbors would write books about what a defective neighbor I was.

And then, of course, if my fame were sufficient, Kitty Kelley herself or Albert Goldman (who did Elvis) or Laurence Leamer (Johnny Carson) would trace every step I ever took and really ream me.

So who needs all that?

Obscurity is so much safer and cozier than fame.

Failure looks better every day.

Besides, fame has other unpleasant drawbacks.

The National Enquirer runs unflattering pictures of you and says you're sneaking around with Elizabeth Taylor or secretly married to all the sopranos in the Mormon Tabernacle Choir.

People magazine insists on taking a humiliating picture of you taking a bubble bath, smoking a cigar and looking overly pleased with yourself.

Your agent insists, despite your protests, that you spend a little time once in a while with the despicable, not to mention inexplicable, David Letterman.

Spy magazine starts calling you a phony and runs a photograph of you with your eyes crossed and lips puckered, even though you can't remember ever doing either maneuver in your life.

Who needs all that grief, right?

I think people are going to become so reluctant to get rich, famous and powerful that they'll start spending enormous amounts of time and energy to avoid becoming too successful.

They will pass up opportunities to make money. Rather than read self-help books, they will read self-destruct books on how to avoid success by making bad investments and keeping away from people who can help them. And they will attend special classes on how to develop a worse personality, lose friends and develop and maintain bad breath.

Beautiful people will get cosmetic surgery, have big lumps put on their noses and get fat as rhinoceroses to reduce their chances of ever becoming successful models and actors.

And politicians will go so far as to start telling the truth to avoid advancing too far and becoming too powerful and influential.

Hmmm . . .

Actually, some of these possibilities don't sound so bad, do they?

Thoughts I Couldn't Put a Stop to ...

Don't people seem a little more dignified and interesting when they're in airports?

•

If Emporia would grow south 21 miles and Eureka north 21 miles, the two wildly growing Kansas cities could merge and be renamed Euphoria.

•

Watch out for people who call their hang-ups convictions.

•

I never liked George Burns until he got old.

•

Did the person who created the crossword puzzle get away with it without being punished?

IF ELECTED . . .

*"I believe in today's youth. I just don't want to sit too
close to them in restaurants when they're in large,
silly groups."*

1979

This Isn't Quite How Ted Koppel Does It

November 7, 1984

Downtown Wichita was dark. Stores, offices and even most clubs – for some reason – were closed. Police cars seemed to be everywhere, some parked and watching traffic, some cruising.

It was the night before the election, and getting late.

A young woman in remarkably snug, flashy black slacks strolled north along Broadway, glancing at the traffic that went by.

Nice night for a walk.

Fifty-two degrees, the Kansas State Bank and Trust building said.

The Blue Lounge and Koma Lounge on so-called skid row, the Looking Glass, Wendy's and Jax were all dark. The Eaton Hotel lobby was empty.

But McDonald's was open – till midnight – and around 11, a man who had been driving around downtown went in for a cup of coffee.

Only one other customer was inside, a woman a little too made-up.

Maybe five minutes later, the woman in the remarkably snug, flashy slacks and another young woman arrived, got coffee, and sat down.

The man had been looking for an offbeat election eve story. Maybe this was a little too offbeat, but . . .

Flashy Slacks looked over at him. He picked up his coffee, walked over and asked, "Mind if I join you?"

"Why not?"

80

Flashy was a good-looking black woman who had her hair in an elegant kind of style, pulled up and off her neck. But her eyes were red, and she looked sort of permanently tired. On her blouse she wore a button that said, "I AMAZE MYSELF."

The other woman was white, young in a waiflike way, and wearing dark glasses. Her eyes were badly bruised and swollen.

"Nice night to get out and get some fresh air, isn't it?" the man asked.

"Sure is," parried Flashy.

"I'm with the newspaper, The Eagle," the man said right away. "Like to get your names in the paper? Get famous?"

"The newspaper?" asked Flashy, frowning and lighting a Kool.

"I'm seeing what the atmosphere is like downtown the night before the election. Except I can't find any. Want to talk politics?"

The man felt like Ted Koppel.

Flashy pounced on the question: "If I was gonna vote, I'd vote for Mondale. But he's not gonna win. He ain't gotta chance."

Dark Glasses said, "Reagan's too old."

Flashy said, "Reagan's makin' the rich richer and the poor poorer."

"He's gettin' senile," Dark Glasses said. "You can tell, watching him on TV."

"I never vote," Flashy said. "Don't make any sense to. All the good presidents got killed. The Kennedys. There never gonna be another good one."

Both women came to town Sunday by bus from Albuquerque, they said. To visit a friend.

Dark Glasses said she'd been in a car wreck. Banged her

81

head hard. Had to have some stitches in her scalp.

"She coulda been killed," Flashy said.

Dark Glases nodded.

I asked if they knew about the crackdown on streetwalkers and johns not long ago – not that it had anything to do with them.

"No, but I ain't doin' nothin'," Flashy said. "Just came here to visit my girlfriend. And I got bored so I'm takin' a walk."

"You dressed nice to take your walk," the man said.

"Thank you."

The woman sitting alone in the restaurant left.

"Sure a lot of female impersonators in Wichita," Flashy said.

"How's that?"

"What? You didn't see that one?"

"The . . . the woman or whatever who just left?"

"Woman, hunnnh! You couldn't tell?"

A transvestite in McDonald's. Have it your way.

"One transvestite doesn't make a lot, though," the man said.

"I counted six on the streets tonight," Flashy said with authority, lighting another Kool.

It was getting late. The man said he had to go.

"Be good," Flashy said.

"Take care," he said.

The man went home and opened a beer.

"How'd it go?" his wife asked.

"Hmmmm. Well, ah, I guess you could say I found two people who aren't going to vote for Reagan."

Now May I Ask You This, Sir: *Huh?*

November 28, 1979

I used to think that my difficulty understanding Sen. Edward Kennedy during TV interviews was my fault.

I assumed that my mind simply wasn't quick enough to follow Kennedy's brilliant, maze-like answers.

But a recent William Buckley column pointed out that others find Kennedy something less than articulate during interviews, as opposed to how forcefully he comes across giving speeches.

Buckley cited this exchange from an interview by CBS' Roger Mudd on Nov. 2:

Mudd: Why do you want to be president?

Kennedy: Well, I'm . . . were I to make the announcement to run, the reasons that I would run is because I have a great belief in this country, that it is . . . there's more natural resources than any nation of the world; there's the greatest educated population in the world; greatest technology of any country in the world, and the greatest political system in the world.

"And the energies and the resourcefulness of this nation, I think, should be focused on these problems in a way that brings a sense of restoration . . . in this country by its people to . . . in dealing with the problems we face. Primarily the issues of . . . energy. And . . . I would basically feel that . . . that it's imperative for this country to either move forward; that it can't stand still or otherwise it moves backward."

I'm not singling Kennedy out here because he's any more befuddling than other candidates. I'm doing it because when I read that answer, it hit me, I can talk like that. I imagined myself holding a press conference to announce my candidacy for the presidency:

Roger Mudd: Mr. Getz, why do you feel that you're qualified to be president?

Mr. Getz: Because I am absolutely positive, that is, confident, which is to say, the country is in trouble . . . there's Iran; there's inflation . . . what the people of this country want is a leader with a sense of direction. Next question?

Sam Donaldson: You have no political experience whatsoever, Mr. Getz. Do you honestly believe that the voters will support you?

Mr. Getz: It is not a question of . . . the people will support the candidate they think . . . we live in the greatest country in the world. We have the resourcefulness, we have the imagination, we have the technology . . . all we need is the leadership. We can either take the bull by the horns, or, to get back to your question, that's the way I see it.

Peter Jennings: Do you feel, then, as I suppose you must, that you're the most qualified candidate? And why?

Mr. Getz: Let me answer those two questions one at a time. First, I am extremely mindful that as we move into the 1980s, we have to come to grips . . . for example, my mother has worked hard all her life. On the other hand, I believe prosperity is just around the corner if only we have the best man in the White House. There are no two ways about it, and the time has come for such candor.

Mudd: What would you do about Iran?

Mr. Getz: The situation there is very delicate . . . it calls for boldness, decisive action and diplomacy. The United States cannot allow itself to be pushed around, and it should do nothing drastic. The eyes of the world are on us.

84

Jennings: What about the energy problems?

Mr. Getz: Vision and imagination have been clearly lacking in American government for . . . the people are tired and worried. It's time for action, not rhetoric. I would take three decisive steps. I would (a), well, the country must be prepared to expect certain, that is, within three years, I know we can see the light at the end of the tunnel. Americans are tired of waiting, and they deserve action now!

Donaldson: Do you think you can win the election?

Mr. Getz: I have faith in the American people. I believe . . . I know they will make the right decision, the decision that is best for America, once they understand who I am, where I am going, and what, exactly, I can do for them.

How to Win Elections – and Pick Up Women

December 20, 1987

So Gary Hart, the dauntless not to mention moneyless, staffless and apparently rudderless presidential candidate, is at it again.

What a guy. Hart seems determined to prove a political campaign can be the moral equivalent of a practical joke – insulting, disgusting, yet perversely amusing.

Good for him.

A little wacky humor never hurt any presidential sweepstakes.

Hart may very well be redefining political campaigning. The way Gary Hart runs for president, he really ought to use a cigar as a prop and have two or three funny brothers to honk horns and chase skirts with.

The way Gary Hart runs for president, he needs a short, fat running mate with a name like Costello or Hardy, or pals named Curley and Moe who are good at saying yuk-yuk-yuk and hitting each other over the head with a rubber mallet.

Vaudeville isn't dead, it has just been recycled as 1980s politics, Gary Hart-style.

This isn't democracy in action, it's burlesque. When Hart stumps the campaign trail, he should come up with a whole show.

He could be preceded by a juggler, a dog act, a comedian, a stripper – *Annnd now, for your entertainment and political pleasure, here he is, our main attraction, the star of the show, the man we all love to read about in the tabloids, doing his incredible imitation of a decent human being running for president like nobody ever ran for president before, the one, the only, GARRRRR-rrry HARRRT!*

But enough of this mirth, frivolity and good-natured kidding around. Let's get mean. No, no. Actually, let's be helpful.

Gary Hart says he has no money with which to become our 41st president. How touching. So I would like to offer Hart a suggestion.

All he has to do to make big bucks is write a book that would appeal to the masses, or at least to all the National Enquirer readers, called "How to Win Friends and Elections, Influence People Into Contributing to Your Campaign and Pick Up Women."

And here, for Sen. Hart's inspiration, are some suggested chapters and "excerpts" he might use in his book:

How to Campaign in Iowa
and Still Have Some Fun

"Iowa is a dull but somehow important state. You need to show up, shake everybody's hand, pose in feed caps and pretend you like farming and pigs. Iowa's idea of nightlife is watching Triple A baseball, but it is possible to have fun there if you know where to look. So for a good time in Iowa, dial 090-1234 in Des Moines and ask for Lola."

How to Enlist Idealistic
Youth as Campaign Workers

1. Tell her that you are a candidate of vision with great ideas.

2. Share your great ideas with her.

3. If she doesn't slap your face when she hears your great ideas, ask her about her views on Bimini.

4. If she still lacks enthusiasm for your ideas, tell her you know Warren Beatty personally and if she's a loyal campaign worker, you'll introduce them and maybe he can find a little part in a movie for her.

Lines for Picking Up Women
in Campaign Offices, Bars, etc.

"My political party doesn't understand me."

"Hi, beautiful. My name is Gary, and I don't believe in small talk. My yacht or yours?"

"What's a nice girl like you doing in a campaign like this?"

"How'd you like to come up and see my campaign posters?"

Lines to Use Upon
Encountering Resistance

If she says: "Get lost, Buster!"

You say: "Excuse me, but I take it you don't know who I am. A thousand pardons for not introducing myself before I made a pass at you, but you should have said, 'Get lost, Mr. 41st President!' "

If she says: "OK, look, I'll have one more drink, OK? But it's after midnight and I really have to go. And, by the way: Why are all those people with notebooks and TV cameras hanging around outside?"

You say: "What? Who are you, lady? How did you get in here? Help! Police! A burglar!"

All yours, Gary. Happy *campaigning* (wink!).

———

Being Nice to Donna Rice

June 21, 1987

Did you catch Barbara Walters' exclusive "interview" with Donna Rice the other night? You didn't? Sorry I didn't tape it for you then. I'm afraid I don't remember how it went, exactly. But just for you, I'll do the best I can here and, based on my impressions of what was and wasn't said, make something up. . . .

"Hello, evwybody! I'm Baa-baa Walters, and this is Donna Wice. Donna, by the way, isn't being paid for this interview, and considering how it will go, I pwobably shouldn't be paid for it, either.

"Now, Donna, I just want you to welax and say anything you darned well please, however silly, presumptuous and self-serving, for the next 30 minutes, while I sit here and look infinitely and curiously sympathetic. And don't worry your pwetty little head that I might ask you any tough questions, OK?"

"OK, Barbara. I just wish all journalists were as nice as you!"

"Well, tell us, Donna. How you holding up?"

"This has been rough, Barbara, just the worst time of my life – even worse than the tragic time I broke my nail right before my senior prom! Oh, boo-hoo, boo-hoo, some things are just so hard to get over!"

"Donna, why don't you tell us a little about yourself?"

"What's there to tell, Barbara? I'm simply a nice girl, a typical fox-next-door-who'd-like-to-be-in-the-movies. I've held a respectable job in a big, honest company. And I was an honor student, even if you'd never guess, listening to the way I talk and think.

"And so what, I say, if I've dated some stars, encountered some playboys and attended some swinging parties in Aspen and L.A. – who hasn't? A girl can't sit home knitting every night, right?"

"I hear that since all this happened, you got an agent, Donna."

"Oh, you know how it is. What else could I do? If my life is going to be in shambles and my poor, dear family shamed and humiliated, I think I'm obligated to try to salvage a successful movie or modeling career out of it, don't you?"

"Tell me, Donna. What have you learned from this experience?"

"Oh, something very important, Barbara! From now on, I'll always find out whether married men I hardly know who ask me out on yachts are presidential candidates or not! I've learned my lesson!

"Another thing I've learned is how awful the media are! They're despicable! I think it's a sad day for this country when a married presidential candidate, whose campaign emphasis is on restoring integrity, trust and honor to the White House, can't go out on a little overnight cruise with a willowy blond model without the media getting all carried away. It's a shame Gary dropped out. He's neat, you know."

"What did you think of your friend's article in People?"

"It just proves you can't trust anybody, Barbara – even people you've known for months. It will be a cold day in

July before I ever sit in a presidential candidate's lap again and let somebody take our picture!

"And you know, Barbara, I heard that People paid Lynn Armandt around $150,000! Doesn't that explain everything? She just said that stuff for the money, it's as simple as that!"

"But wouldn't she have been paid the same money, no matter what she said in the story?"

"Could you edit that insensitive remark out, please, Barbara? It sounds just like a question the awful media would ask!"

"Did you know Gehwy Hart was married?"

"Oh, I think it came up, but he didn't really go into details, you know."

"Well, Donna. I guess I must ask The Question. Did you get intimately involved with Gehwy Hart that night?"

"I won't answer that, as a matter of dignity."

"Are you sure you wouldn't rather lie, Donna? Your answer sure sounds like a cautious, undignified 'yes' to me."

"Could you edit that remark out, too, please, Barbara?"

"Well, Donna. If, as Lynn Armandt said, you weren't with her that night, could you have been out on the deck alone, fishing all night?"

"I'm sorry, Barbara. I'm just not the kind of girl who fishes and tells. But I will tell our audience one thing."

"What's that?"

"My new agent's phone number."

May I Speak to a World Leader, Please?

October 8, 1986

Forget fantasy. Forget flights of fancy. Who needs that stuff?

Forget fiction, fables, fairy tales, myths and all those other reliably delightful varieties of lies.

Sometimes real life is enough.

Take the other day. A strange phone call happened to me.

It was from a fine earthling named Bob Guessford.

"Do you want a good idea for your column?" he asked.

Well. That depends. Even I have my standards.

"Try to call a world leader."

What?

"Try to call a world leader and see if you can get through. You can't get through."

The man sounded sober enough. Sober, sincere, even earnest.

"I tried to get through to a world leader in August, and I couldn't," Guessford said.

Which world leader?

"Quite a few. You can't even talk to Bob Dole."

Who all did you try to call?

"President Reagan. Gorbachev. The president of France. The presidents of Italy and Mexico. Queen Elizabeth. The only one I got through to was the president of Zaire. He called me 'Mr. American.' "

The president of Zaire called you Mr. American? When did you make all these calls?

91

"One day in August. I did it because I'm just sitting out here in Wichita, Kansas, and I thought, 'I'd like to talk to a world leader.' Just to see if I could. But you can't. My phone bill that month was $500."

So what happened when you tried to call Reagan?

"I talked to one of his secretaries. She asked me what I wanted. I said, 'I just want to say, "How in the heck are things going, Ron?" ' She said, 'The president's too busy.' "

Well, world leaders are pretty busy people.

"I'm retired Air Force. Fifty-six years old. I met a lot of VIPs in the world."

But if you were a world leader, would you talk to any Tom, Ricardo or Sergei who called you up?

"Sure would. If I had the time. That's where you get all your information, talking to people."

What were you going to say to the world leaders?

"When I called Gorbachev, I was going to say, 'How's it going, Mike? How the hell's it going?' His name is Mike, right?"

Sort of. Mikhail, I think.

"Well, it would help if world leaders talked to common people. If we can't talk to them, how they gonna understand us? And you know what? Sometimes somebody's got to relieve the tension. Just make a friendly phone call."

I laughed. Call and share a smile with Mikhail.

"It's impossible to talk to a world leader, though. You can't talk to the president, you can't talk to Dan Glickman, you can't talk to Dole. With all these secretaries, you can't get through to them. This world is getting too serious, Bob. Sometimes I worry about it."

So what did the president of Zaire (Sese Seko Mobutu) have to say?

"He said, 'Hello, Mr. American. What can I do for you?' I said I just wanted to call and say hello and ask how the heck he was doing. He said, 'Everything's just fine. How's everything with you?' I said, 'It's raining like hell over here.' He said, 'Our rainy season doesn't start for another three months.' "

Sounds like a nice guy. Especially for a world leader.

"You know, I read an article last week on the 55 speed limit by Mike Royko of the Chicago Tribune syndicate. I liked it, so I thought, 'I'll just call up his office and tell him.'

"You know what? You can't even talk to him! He has a male secretary who asks a thousand questions. I said, 'Is he in?' He said, 'Yeah.' I said, 'Hey, can I talk to him?' He said, 'No.' "

I told Guessford I had to write a column about him.

"I don't know. I think you ought to try to call a world leader sometime."

Maybe I will. If . . .

"Hey, I gotta go, buddy. I got another call coming in."

Another call? Maybe it was Ron calling back.

———

Play the Primary Game; Everyone's a Winner!

March 14, 1984

Saying "uncle" is never easy.

Especially when you're running for a really good job like the presidency of the United States.

If you're a presidential candidate and you lose a primary or a caucus, the last thing you want to do is talk or act like you lost.

No matter how resoundingly you're defeated, you must proclaim the loss as some sort of major triumph – and sound half convincing.

It is not good form, upon finishing lower than first in a primary, to weep, wring one's hands, rend one's garments, tear one's hair and scream at the top of one's lungs, "God, what a pathetic showing. I'm going to go get drunk!"

Instead you say:

"We *won* 0.5 of the vote in Iowa, and now we've *won* a full 1 percent in New Hampshire! This is the kind of strong showing we were hoping for. Our campaign is gaining momentum! Clearly, more Americans are beginning to get my message! Ultimate victory will be ours!"

Some might say this is the Power of Presumptuous Poppycock.

It's not whether you win or lose that counts, it's what you say afterward that really matters. You hope.

For instance, say you're a candidate in a six-man primary. Here's how you would handle any particular finish:

First – "This was one of the most important primaries to win! Winning here proves I am the candidate of the people, a man of destiny, and the only guy in the field worth his salt!"

Second – "This is as good as winning – if not better! We figured Candidate A would win, considering he has two cousins – *first* cousins – here and is virtually a favorite son. But he won with only 83 percent when we anticipated he'd get at least 90! So I think we can virtually claim an upset victory here!"

Third – "This is wonderful! Our goal was fourth. My campaign is ripening ahead of schedule!"

Fourth – "Our goal here was just to beat Candidate F, but we also beat Candidate E! We're on our way!"

Fifth – "I'm delighted. We did minimal campaigning

here and yet we beat Candidate F. Obviously, there is a groundswell going on for me, and it's a beautiful thing! Just two weeks ago, not even my wife knew my name, and now six people have voted for me! No doubt about it, we've got Candidate A running scared now!"

Sixth – "I'm encouraged. Considering the demographics of this state, the weather today, the phase of the moon, and the lies everybody has been telling about me, I think we did much better than we might have hoped for. This was a very strong last-place finish, and I predict it will provide us with the impetus my campaign needs to take off!"

When he was in a real bind, John Paul Jones once commented, "I have not yet begun to fight!"

Presidential candidates say about the same thing when they're on the ropes.

After John Glenn finished a weak sixth in Iowa, he said, "I hope we will resist the temptation to blow what happened out of proportion."

But John. East is east, and sixth is sixth.

George McGovern said his "third" in Iowa was "a minor miracle."

Sometimes you get the feeling that if some politicians were boxers who had just been beaten to a pulp, they'd manage to mumble, "Why should I feel bad? I finished second, didn't I? A major miracle."

In Iowa, Alan Cranston said he "had" to finish third.

He came in fourth.

And he boasted, "My unavowed hope was to defeat John Glenn, and I did."

I also greatly admired what one member of the Mondale team said after Walter lost in New Hampshire: "We are energized by this."

I wonder what Custer's last words were.

"We are energized by this"? "I have not yet begun to

fight"? "We may have been massacred, but I think we did well enough to claim a moral victory"? or, "I hope history will resist the temptation to blow what happened out of proportion"?

And so yesterday was "Super Tuesday."

I can hardly wait to read what all the non-losers had to say – before they slinked off to the bathroom and bawled their eyes out.

————

Go, Grads! Go Be Happy and Harmless!

May 28, 1989

For some mysterious, unfathomable reason, I am sometimes asked to give graduation-type speeches. To provide commencement babble and such for various graduation rites.

I decline.

I'm flattered to be asked, of course. But I simply don't know why anybody would risk asking me to deliver such a significant address, even though nobody really pays that much attention to this glorified drivel anyway, unless, of course, a school is lucky enough to get Jane Pauley, Kim Basinger or somebody acceptably strange and contemporary such as Bon Jovi or Manuel Noriega.

One of the major reasons I refuse to subject any defenseless graduates to my thoughts is that I say enough dumb things in the course of the average day as it is without going out of my way to do it some more on an occasion when I might even be taken seriously.

Why I get these invitations, I don't know.

Maybe I accidentally wrote something once that almost made sense, so a few people got the wrong impression and jumped to the outrageous conclusion that I might be able to do it again sometime.

Zounds.

No way would I inflict a commencement address on anyone.

Let someone else far more qualified than I have the last desperate shot at inspiring graduates.

Let someone else much deeper emotionally and intellectually than I, and much more skilled at keeping a straight face, get up and chant the usual trite, true, snooze-inducing cliches.

I can think of much more convivial places where I can go to spout my nonsense at scowling, bored strangers.

Besides, how could I ever forgive myself if I gave a commencement spiel and somehow actually inspired some students to go on to lead shameless lives of politics, TV writing or journalism?

Whatever, kids sure don't need me. Unlike some of my hysterical peers, I have every confidence that today's American youth will be the best generation that has come down the pike.

I believe in them. I have faith in them.

I just don't want to sit too close to them in restaurants when they're in large, silly groups.

But can you believe the way some of today's grown-ups wring their hands with concern over whether today's and tomorrow's kiddies will be up to handling the country? About whether they'll be as well-qualified as past generations?

Hahahahaha – right?

Think about it.

Look what a mess our generations have made of this

planet, and we're worried about the next generation not being up to snuff?

I just have no doubt that today's youth, maybe even the ones who cut their hair so strange and nerdy, will take great strides toward fixing, tuning up, overhauling and improving this wobbly, creaking, overheating, backfiring, banged-up planet.

This isn't to say these graduates' future doesn't look bleak.

It does. As much as I hate to say it, today's graduates can expect a scary future in that many of them will no doubt live a life of Rotary meetings, Junior League teas, lost baggage, company picnics, interminable cocktail parties where they can't find anybody on their wavelength, bent fenders and various kinds of excruciating meetings.

Other than that, though, young people, I have faith that you all will do just terrific, become everything you need to be and want to be, or, failing that, you'll at least be halfway happy and harmless.

But what, you might actually be wondering, would I seriously say in a commencement speech to graduates who are sitting slouched in their seats, obviously raring to go and eager to get on with their lives, conquer the world and do some serious partying that night?

Don't get drunk and killed. And don't go riding with somebody else who's sloshed and get yourself annoyingly dead.

Death tends to foul up even the most promising futures.

That isn't profound. But it's probably about as wise as I can get.

Anyway. Congratulations, 1989 graduates. And may I leave you on this possibly depressing, even horrifying note, a quote from rock 'n' roll relic Frank Zappa (Dweezil and Moon's deliriously observant dad):

"The older you get, the more you realize life is like high school."

How Would Media Handle Armageddon?

August 27, 1990

Wouldn't you know it? Just when I finally get my car paid off, people start saying the world could end soon.

Did you see that story in the paper Saturday – "Mideast tension sparks fear of Armageddon"?

Hoo, boy.

Some seem to think, based on what the Bible says, that the end, Judgment Day, could happen any minute now.

That ought to make some kids happy.

No school this year.

Or ever again.

Unless they have school in heaven.

But how could anybody say heaven is nice if it has schools?

I digress.

Moving right along . . . Obviously there is a showdown of showdowns going on there in the biblical land of the Middle East, and it's even worse than any Sunday school teacher may have ever told you.

That is: Gathered there now for one great battle are the major evil TV forces known to us as CBS, NBC and ABC, and they have all their big guns – Brokaw, Koppel, Donaldson and Rather – ready for one mighty ratings confrontation.

Whatever that means, could this be it?

99

Genuine Armageddon? The end? Judgment Day? The day of reckoning?

I shudder to think how some people will react if The End happens.

Will Koppel lose his cool?

Will Sam Donaldson play tough and belligerently demand of God, "What's this nonsense about the *meek* inheriting the Earth?"

Will Walter Cronkite be hauled out of retirement and rushed to the scene on special assignment, and will God be the least bit impressed?

Will newspaper editors cry out for forgiveness and mercy – or drive their staffs even harder to get out one really Final edition?

Will any journalists at all get to go to heaven?

Any lawyers? Any politicians?

Will the S&L hustlers and politicians try to cut a deal with God to get into heaven?

Will wackos like Michael Jackson, Madonna and Roseanne Barr try to charm God into letting them into heaven by rubbing their crotches?

Will drug dealers and gang members insist they get into heaven because they're so cool, and when God laughs, pull guns on him, making him roll on the clouds, laughing even harder?

Ah, Armageddon. Talk of it brings back the memories.

Like many other lucky kids, I grew up hearing an awful lot about Judgment Day. At least I did whenever I stayed with my very religious grandparents and uncle.

They were all such genuinely good, kind, God-fearing people that they scared me silly.

They always believed things were so bad that the world just had to end any minute. That God couldn't take it anymore. And they *liked* the idea.

I didn't. I was only 10. I wanted to hide behind chairs.

They'd sit around studying the Bible and discussing the importance of being perfect and belonging to the Right Church, while I, a little kid who'd never done anything much worse in life than steal second base, would sit nearby, listening, worried sick that the world would end and I'd not only not get to go to heaven, but, worse, would miss out on the rest of the Little League season.

And all I can say now, as a middle-aged guy, is, well, what an awful time in my life to have to think about starting to be nice so I can go to heaven. I know too much now to want to be sweet.

Ah, well. I guess I can always look at the bright side:

If the world ends any minute, I get out of paying off my credit cards.

Getting Away
From It All

April 29, 1987

"I can't take it anymore," my friend Bofko muttered, staring despairingly down into the murky depths of his citrus wine cooler.

"I have to get away from it all," he wheezed. "It's really getting to me. The scandals. The hypocrisy. The hype. The nonsense."

"Where do you want to go, Bofko?" I asked. "Hawaii? Acapulco?"

"To a cave somewhere in the wilderness!" Bofko snapped. "To some place where you never hear about every body's drug problems and Oliver North and

Geraldo Rivera!"

"That sounds great, Bofko. Except then you might miss seeing Vanna White's movie debut."

Glaring at me, Bofko said, "A cave in the Rockies might be nice. Just think! No more news of Jim and Tammy! No more nonsense!"

"I know what you mean, Bofko," I said. "That stuff gets me down sometimes, too. Some nights I can't even handle the weather forecast."

"I want to live in a cave out someplace where I can lie on my back, stare at the sky, read and maybe think a little when I'm feeling particularly daring."

"That's nice, Bofko. But aren't caves awfully damp and gloomy? And what about snakes and all those slimy bugs that love moisture?"

"You've got a point. If I'm going to spend the rest of my life in the wilderness, there's no point dying of pneumonia or snakebite the first night. I'll take a tent."

"A tent is fun for a few days, Bofko. But if you live in one all the time, you'll probably end up freezing to death."

"Good thinking. So the only solution is a cabin. I'll live in a crude cabin in the mountains far from any news of silly humanity."

"That sounds good. But if you're far from any news of humanity, how are you going to keep up with the humanity on the Cardinals?"

"Hmmm. I guess I could make one concession. I'll take a radio. And lots of batteries. But just to get Cards' baseball scores."

"You can't trust radio for sports, Bofko. Public Radio might tell you the entire history of sumo wrestling, but just try getting a simple St. Louis baseball score on a station. Especially out in the wilderness."

"You've got a point. The rest of my life is going to be a

long time, so maybe I should find a place that's not quite so remote I can't use a TV set. But just for games. And maybe presidential elections."

"That's good, Bofko. And if you had electricity for a TV, you could have a refrigerator, too. That would really simplify how you keep your food fresh – all the creatures you shoot. The deer and rabbits."

"I don't want to shoot any deer and rabbits."

"You going to live on nuts and berries and fish?"

"Geez. Actually, if I live close enough to civilization to have electricity, I could probably make trips into some town sometimes to get essential supplies like TV dinners, soup, toilet paper and an occasional carryout pizza. Do you think I could find a crude cabin like that somewhere? With indoor plumbing?"

"Sure. But then you'll get utility bills, you know. Have you saved up enough money to pay bills and buy supplies for the rest of your life?"

"Heck, no. Maybe I could find a part-time job and just drive back and forth to the wilderness. Besides, what would happen if I was living too far out in the wilderness and got terribly sick?"

"Or ran out of beer."

"Right."

"Bofko? I can think of only one solution."

"What?"

"I know a nice house for sale five miles out of Wichita. It has a hot tub. Luxurious den with a wet bar. Swimming pool. Barbecue pit. Fenced yard for privacy. It's a great place to live and get away from it all. Better than the wilderness. And it has four trees!"

Bofko stared at the wall. What was this sensitive, soulful American man thinking now? No doubt he was struggling to get his '80s' priorities in order, straining to decide

103

how best to survive sensibly in these maddening modern times.

"One important question," he mumbled.

"What's that?"

"Does it have central air?"

_____

Thoughts I Couldn't Put a Stop to . . .

Imagine what a member of a Pia Zadora Fan Club would be like.

•

Why don't we say cake a la mode?

•

Do any ballet dancers ever wear glasses?

•

Good disc jockeys seldom sound sincere.

•

Restaurants ought to give you toast with all breakfasts.

•

Ever wonder how much Imelda Marcos spent on shoe polish?

•

What if all women sounded like Sandy Duncan?

•

Do you think anybody ever called Rachmaninov "Rocky"?

•

Honk if you hate honking.

I ♥ Kansas (Really!)

"People are so jaded anymore — even in Kansas, where you'd think becoming jaded was virtually impossible."

1980

VISIT EXCITING KANSAS! SEE MOODY COW!

June 20, 1982

Our Kansas. Our beloved Kansas. Our beloved, sluggish Kansas.

It doesn't seem to have the foggiest idea how to get anybody to come here and stay awhile and spend some money.

What a state. Month after month, year after year, I open press releases revealing Kansas' latest promotional hype.

That usually means the Department of Tourism has come up with a new slogan. Which usually means that somebody thought up a new pun on the word Oz.

I can't stand it anymore. Oz, Oz, Oz . . .

The state's tourism people seem to think that the secret of luring people to Kansas is to convince them that this is Oz.

Oz, schmoz. I'll tell you what Kansas needs if it's really serious about wanting tourists and travelers to hang around and spend their money here.

Signs.

Lots of signs.

Signs to the right of the roads, signs to the left of the roads, signs facing every direction, and signs on every interstate, on every highway, on every gravel road, and maybe even every driveway. Signs. And billboards.

You see, what has to be done is to arouse the curiosity of travelers to such a feverish pitch that they'll forget all about going on to Colorado Springs and the Ozarks. Make people want to follow signs to satisfy their incredibly inflamed curiosity.

Billboards and signs will do that.

You take states such as Tennessee, California, Georgia and Florida. Now there are four states that really know the power of signs.

Kansas? Kansas only really seems to believe in two kinds of signs, ones that carry either one of these two enchanting messages: (1) Santa Fe Trail Historical Marker 1,000 feet, and (2) Picnic Table 1,000 Feet.

But in, say, Tennessee, you see signs, signs, signs:

FIREWORKS!!! 50 MILES!!! FIREWORKS – 49 MILES!!! FIREWORKS – 43 MILES!!!

If at first you yawn at such signs, by the time you have seen one every half-mile for 50 miles, when you finally get close to the shops and booths that are advertised, you're ready to kill, if necessary, to get some fireworks – pity the poor fellow traveler who gets in your way – and if you aren't, your kids are.

Then take Georgia and Florida: ALLIGATOR WRESTLING – 572 MILES!!!

Why, by the time you read the 47,552nd and final sign, you are so psyched up for some alligator wrestling that you're almost ready to take on those danged gators yourself.

So must it be, then, in Kansas.

Chambers of Commerce of Kansas, arise and unite! Kansas Department of Tourism? Merchants? Are you paying attention? Some suggestions:

WILD BUFFALO WRESTLING – 410 MILES!!! GIANT UNTAMED BUFFALO WRESTLING – 409 MILES!!! MAN-EATING BUFFALO WRESTLING – JUST 408 MILES!!! Etc.

The possibilities are endless:

THE WORLD'S LARGEST MAN-EATING BALL OF TWINE – 285 MILES!!! FEROCIOUS GIANT BALL OF TWINE-WRESTLING – 265 MILES!!!

VISIT EXCITING TOPEKA & THE WORLD'S WILDEST, MOST VICIOUS, MAN-EATING ANTIQUE CAR – 370 MILES!!!

SEE THE WORLD'S SICKEST, MOST DEPRAVED HUMOR – VISIT EARTH'S WILDEST CITY – DODGE CITY – AND READ THE WORLD'S FUNNIEST TOMB-STONE EPITAPHS!!! – 410 MILES!!!

VISIT JESSE JAMES' HIDEOUT – IF YOU DARE!!! SEE WHERE THE VICIOUS, NOTORIOUS OUTLAW USED TO HIDE A LOT!!! WITH LUCK, IT MAY EVEN BE OPEN!!! – 93 MILES!!!

WILD, MAN-EATING PRAIRIE-DOG WRESTLING – 255 MILES!!!

SEE MEL'S DEADLY REPTILES, KILLER SQUIR-RELS, WILD CHICKENS, MEAN GARTER SNAKE, HAZARDOUS WASTE DUMP & SOUVENIR SHOP – 202 MILES!!!

IF YOU CAN STAND IT, VISIT DANGEROUS, INCREDIBLE, BREATHTAKING LITTLE HOUSE ON THE PRAIRIE!!! – ALSO SEE A VERY MOODY COW THAT'S KEPT IN THE BACK YARD!!! – 401 MILES!!!

Then there would be one more advantage to having thousands of such billboards and signs up. They could kind of hide the state so travelers would be less likely to fall asleep while driving to all those exciting tourist hot spots.

———

Real Kansas Men Never Even Heard of Quiche

August 9, 1982

By popular demand (which is to say, somebody asked), I have taken it upon myself to do a localized or Kansas-ized takeoff on "Real Men Don't Eat Quiche," the great new book by Bruce Feirstein which I gave you a dose of last week.

To refresh your memory, the book said Real Men are guys like Elvis Presley, Pete Rose, Jane Pauley and Robert Mitchum, while Quiche Eaters are types like Dick Cavett, Chevy Chase, Halston and Burt Bacharach.

I thought localizing the idea would be a snap. But when I actually got down to doing it, I made a startling discovery:

Very few of our better-known Kansans seem to qualify, by the book's high standards, as Quiche Eaters. Thank God.

But, never one to let reality, facts and other such annoying obstacles get in the way of a column idea, I just gave the "Real Men Don't Eat Quiche" a little twist and came up with . . .

• Real Kansas Men go to rodeos. Quiche Eaters go to Cowtown.

• Real Kansas Men go to the Circle Cinema Adult Art Theater. Quiche Eaters go to art museums.

• Quiche Eaters go to symphonies. Real Kansas Men go to Joyland Amusement Park.

• Real Kansas Men never miss the state fair. Quiche Eaters think state fairs ought to be outlawed.

• Real Kansas Men pronounce quiche as KISH-ee, not keesh. Real Kansas Men who have class pronounce it kish-SHAY.

• For a big night out, Real Kansas Men take their women to a drive-in movie – on a combine.

• Real Kansas Men idolize Clint Eastwood. Quiche Eaters idolize Peter Lawford.

• A Real Kansas Man's idea of fun is watching mud wrestling. A Quiche Eater's idea of fun is sitting down front at a school board meeting.

• Real Kansas Men play tennis – but only in long pants

and heavy work shoes.

• Real Kansas Men think you don't have a sense of humor unless you have at least two bumper stickers on your car, pickup, van or forehead.

• Real Kansas Men have rifle racks on their pickup trucks – and their cars, *and* their lawn mowers.

• Real Kansas Men wear plaid shirts – with their tuxes when they get married.

• Real Kansas Men don't play video games. They still play pinball, pool (but not bumper pool) and Foosball.

• Real Kansas Men never have Roman numerals after their names.

• Real Kansas Men hate mascots like the San Diego Chicken at sports events – but they think Krazy George is funny.

• A Real Kansas Man's idea of a perfect birthday present for his wife is a dirt bike.

• Real Kansas Men *like* potholes.

And now:

• Gov. John Carlin eats quiche – but only because it's a dairy product.

• Gubernatorial candidate Sam Hardage also eats quiche – but only because he says, "Anything Carlin can do, I can do better."

• Wichita City Commissioner Albert Kirk ate quiche at least once, too – you can still still see some of it in his beard.

• KAKE sportcaster Paul Crane will eat quiche – but only with plenty of ketchup on it.

• Metropolitan Area Planning Commissioner Dave Bayouth thinks quiche is something you call the exterminators in to spray for.

• Police Chief Richard LaMunyon thinks quiche is just the way some people he knows pronounce the word "keys" after they've had a couple of drinks.

110

• Defeated gubernatorial candidate and good-ole-boy Jim Bob Montgomery thinks quiche rhymes with twitch.

• KAKZ's Gene Rump, being a disc jockey who will try anything silly once, wants to be reincarnated as quiche.

• Sheriff Johnnie Darr doesn't know what quiche is, but he thinks he either shot one once, or gave it a deputy's card.

• County Commissioner Tom Scott refuses to eat quiche – but only because he heard fellow commissioner Don Gragg does.

• And former District Attorney Vern Miller won't touch the stuff – in fact, he used to arrest anybody who did.

———

Love Those Real Kansas Women

September 8, 1982

A woman named Liz Johnson wants to get me into trouble. Bad trouble.

She thinks it's only fair that I follow up my "Real Kansas Man" column with one about "Real Kansas Women."

What the heck. I'm game. I only regret, in fact, that I have but one life to give for my newspaper.

Besides, somebody ought to write something to make up for that wire-service story in the paper Monday, "A Guide to the Real Woman."

That is, judging by that article, I think the Denver Post and Chicago Tribune, by pooling their outmoded, chauvinistic attitudes, could set the women's movement back 100 years – or maybe even clear back to the year of Phyllis Schlafly's choice.

Whatever. My turn:

• Real Kansas Women not only don't mind going out on formal dates in a pickup, they want to drive.

• A Real Kansas Woman's idea of ecstasy is being in K mart when a 10-minute blue light discount special is announced.

• Real Kansas Women are proud of the meat on their bones and worry about the health of the skinny models they see in magazines and on TV.

• Real Kansas Women won their first blue ribbon at a county fair when they were 4 years old, and their first blue ribbon at the state fair when they were 6.

• Real Kansas Women wonder what a nice girl like Rose Stanley is doing, working as an *anchorman*.

• Real Kansas Women make their own bread, jam, clothes, cream, butter, ice cream, cakes, pies, bedspreads, pottery, jewelry, medicine, rugs, carpets and coal gasification plants.

• Real Kansas Women always pay by check, whether buying $874.57 worth of groceries at the supermarket or a pack of gum at the drugstore.

• One reason Real Kansas Women favor tennis shoes is because they go with everything.

• Real Kansas Women worry a lot about Robert Wagner getting serious about "another woman" too soon after Natalie Wood's death.

• Real Kansas Women wonder why, when people in the movies say "ciao" to each other, instead of having chow, they leave each other.

• Real Kansas Women consider any woman who pumps iron weird, but even without doing it themselves or having a woman bodybuilder's physique (which is a lot like boxer Thomas Hearns'), they are stronger and healthier.

• Real Kansas Women still hope Dean Martin and Jerry

Lewis will get back together.

• The Real Kansas Woman's idea of a "woman's drink" is beer *in a glass* instead of a can or bottle.

• Real Kansas Women are flattered if their man holds a door for them, but what they really appreciate is their man holding the ladder for them while they paint the house.

• Real Kansas Women prefer movies that are *real* touching and make you cry (like "Smokey and the Bandit") or that are *real* funny (like "Smokey and the Bandit") or *real* action-packed and exciting (like "Smokey and the Bandit") or, occasionally, *real* sophisticated (like "Hooper").

• Real Kansas Women always have nice souvenir ashtrays from Ponca City displayed prominently in their houses.

• Real Kansas Women have nothing but disdain for anybody who sleeps past 6:30 a.m.

• Real Kansas Women could, in a pinch, knit a nice, warm, practical sweater out of leftover spaghetti.

• Real Kansas Women tell their children that if they study their English and make good enough grades, maybe someday they can get a job with the National Enquirer.

• Real Kansas Women swoon when their men put on their pea-green leisure suits.

• Real Kansas Women, whether discussing the innards of a car, TV set, tractor, combine or spaceship, always know the name of everything and never, ever call any mechanism a doodad, doohinkey, whatchamacallit or thingie.

• Real Kansas Women hope their sons will grow up to be like President Ronald Reagan or at least KAKE-TV meteorologist Jim O'Donnell.

• Real Kansas Women have a terrific sense of humor and would never dream of making a nasty phone call or writing a hostile letter to a newspaper columnist.

Where Were You
June 22, 1989?!?

June 25, 1989

The year is 2008. I am a grandfather now. I have so many grandchildren scurrying around my family tree and living room lamps that I've lost count of exactly how many little direct descendants I actually have.

All the kids are visiting me today. We're having a good time. And I know it's only a matter of time before they ask, as they always do, The Question.

Finally, inevitably, they do:

"Tell us again, Grandpa Bob! Where were you and what were you doing on Thursday, June 22, 1989, when Channel 12 co-anchor Susan Peters became the first woman to hitch a ride in a B-1B bomber?"

As always, whenever anyone asks me The Question, my pulse races, I get goose bumps and have to toss down a nitro tablet to steady my heart.

"Ah, how well I remember that day!" I say. "I was at work that cool, cloudy afternoon when I first heard the historic news. I was midway between the supply cabinet aspirins and the water fountain when I heard the big news announced over a nearby TV."

The kids' eyes widen. They just can't seem to hear this story enough: the day history was made in Wichita and Grandpa was there!

"You know," I say, "there are just some things in our lives we never forget, and I'm sure everybody who lived in Kansas then will always remember where they were and what they were doing when Sue Peters became the first woman passenger on a B-1B. Here, let me show you a list I made of historic events of this same grand magnitude:"

Dec. 17, 1903 – Orville Wright becomes first airplane pilot.

May 20-21, 1927 – Charles Lindbergh first man to fly Atlantic solo.

June 18, 1928 – Amelia Earhart first woman to fly across Atlantic.

July 20, 1969 – Neil Armstrong first man to set foot on moon.

Feb. 7, 1984 – Bruce McCandless first human to float in space.

June 22, 1989 – Wichita KWCH-TV anchorette Sue Peters first woman to catch a ride on B-1B bomber.

"Gee!" squeaks little Bobbi Jane. "You must've been so excited!"

"Yes, indeed. Uncontrollably. You cannot imagine the feelings that coursed through me when, finally, Susan, sounding very historical, hyper and cute, announced: 'Susan Peters. Live on the ground now.' "

"Golly, Grandpa! Tell us more!"

"Well, from what I gathered from Sue's numerous reports, the flight was amazing. Amazing, she said many times. Amazing."

"Did the bomber actually carry bombs?" little Bobby asked.

"Was there a women's rest room on board?" Roberta asked.

"Was it scarier than going on the Orient Express at Worlds of Fun?" Robin asked.

"Susan didn't get into those things," I said. "But her colleague Kevin Nunn did do a cute piece about how good the food is at the Air Force base."

"Were you jealous of Sue Peters, Grandpa?"

"Of course! I wished I'd asked to go up. And I'll bet I could've come up with something just as humorous, if not quite as historic."

"Poor Grandpa. A lifetime in newspapers and not much more to show for it than a runner-up trophy from a media tennis tournament."

"Grandpa, did you realize then what a historic event it was?"

"Sure. I might not have, but, fortunately, Channel 12 played it up big for weeks in advance. Then when it happened, they devoted the whole 5 o'clock news to it, led with it at 6 p.m., and featured it again at 10 with Susan still wearing her flight suit and looking perky, cute, historical and just like the first woman ever to fly in a B-1B. In fact, she looked like she arrived at the station by parachute."

"Uh, Grandpa, I just thought of something. Speaking of how historic that was, uh, did any other woman ever want to go up in a B-1B? Or ask? Or even think it mattered, except for TV ratings? I mean, wasn't what they did like turning a nice, solid, non-news feature story about a plane ride into a great moment in aviation history?"

"Yes. But it was great, dear! Just think! An exclusive historic occasion produced and directed just for its viewers by KWCH-TV!"

––––––

So Kansas Is Flat; What of It?

June 11, 1984

Et tu, Shelby Hearon?
Well, who can blame *tu*?
Everybody else does it, so why not *tu*, too?

116

Everybody who comes to Kansas takes a quick look around, ducks a tornado or two, winces, leaves (flees), and, alas, lambastes the state.

Yawwwn.

Visitors who *do words* for a living are invariably unkind and predictably patronizing after they leave, comb their hair and get the dust out of their ears and typewriters.

Sigh.

"Hey, look, world!" they write. "Look what I just found! Kansas! It's flat and windy! Toto's place! And it's just like the movie, except they have tornado shelters now, and it's *all* in technicolor!"

Whoopee.

You get the feeling after some of these people leave that they think Kansas ought to be fixed, or at the very least, apologized for.

Maybe they think that at our state lines and in our airports, we should change the signs from "welcomes" to apologies, like, "YOU ARE NOW ENTERING KANSAS – SORRY."

Or, "YOU ARE NOW LEAVING KANSAS – PLEASE FORGIVE US."

Or maybe they think warnings would be better: "LOOK OUT! YOU ARE NOW ENTERING KANSAS! THIS IS YOUR LAST CHANCE TO TURN AROUND!"

Personally, the longer I live here, the more I love Kansas. This is a state with hair on its chest. Big, tough, mean. It's no sissy state like Florida, Illinois or California.

Nope, Kansas is Kansas. And, if you don't like it, or if you can't deal with it, tough. That's not Kansas' fault, dude; it's yours.

Actually, that's the way the Department of Tourism ought to advertise: "VISIT KANSAS! – IF YOU DARE!"

Shelby Hearon, last name pronounced Herrin, is an

117

author who did a 30-day tour of duty as writer-in-residence at Wichita State University this spring.

After managing a successful escape from Kansas, she wrote a nice little article for the Dallas Times-Herald about her visit here.

Seems the first day she lectured at WSU, she was interrupted by a rude tornado and ended up in a basement with, unlucky woman, a bad audience. That would sour anyone's impression of a place.

Of that experience, she wrote, " . . . Everybody got up and rushed to the basement to wait for the all-clear. 'Where's Toto?' I had asked, but they all looked blank."

Well, shucky darn, Shelby darlin'. That wit of yours is just too quick – never mind that every witty visitor over age 5 has ad-libbed a similar, equally hilarious little joke about Toto.

Poor Shelby. Not only did people fail to laugh at her lines during tornadoes, but when the time came for her to leave, again she found herself in a basement with another twister warning in effect.

Hearon did make it all the way up to Topeka one day without being chased by a tornado, though.

She wrote, "I . . . passed a sign that said: 'For the next 31 miles you will be passing through the scenic Flint Hills.' After that, I noticed by the side of the road from time to time outcroppings which looked like a half-dozen smashed pencil leads. Period, that was it."

The nerve of that woman! Can you believe her, criticizing our beautiful scenic outcroppings of smashed pencil leads? I just hope she never needs some smashed pencil leads from the Kansas Flint Hills someday. She doesn't deserve any.

But I agree with her about the sign, as I know other Kansans do. It is a stupid sign.

I mean, you don't see signs anywhere else like that. . . .

"For the next 74 miles, you will be winding through the scenic Rocky Mountains."

Or, "For the next 117 feet, you will be driving through beautiful downtown Derby."

Ah, well. Come again, Shelby Hearon, and we'll try to make your stay more pleasant, if not awe-inspiring.

We can't stop the tornadoes, and we can't enlarge the Flint Hills so they're visible to the naked eye. But we'll laugh at your jokes.

———

Jet-Setters Just Love the Kansas State Fair

September 9, 1988

Some people don't like the State Fair.

Can you believe that?

People are so jaded anymore – even here in Kansas, where you'd think becoming jaded was virtually impossible. It must be that people today have just become so satiated with constant, sense-deadening pleasures such as cable TV, Shriner parades, square dancing, Frisbee golf, bowling and Wichita nightlife with all its wet T-shirt contests, that the thrill has gone out of the State Fair for them.

What a shame. The State Fair is a celebration, a pageant, a two-week party, a wonderful rural American orgy of sights, sounds, smells and other strange but generally safe, wholesome sensations having to do with sunburn, prices, lost children and prowling Kansas politicians.

Just don't let anybody tell you the fair isn't sophisticated enough for them.

119

The fair has become so sophisticated that it is almost downright decadent. And I'm not just talking about the vibrating chairs they sell in the Industrial Building.

How about the watermelon seed-spitting contest set for Sunday? Tell me that isn't so disgusting it must be sophisticated.

Or the arm-wrestling. (Don't worry. It's not black-tie.)

And now they have a combine demolition derby! Talk about decadence. Farm boys, when I was a kid, used to get their jollies by crushing beer cans. Now they crush each other's combines. What's more depraved and sophisticated than getting together and smashing your combines?

And if you have any remaining doubts about the sophisticated, cultural nature of the State Fair, I am happy to point out that the sculpted butter exhibit will be at the fair once again. A whole half-ton of butter sculpture, suitable for looking at, spreading on your toast or melting down and pouring over your popcorn.

But don't take my word for how great the Kansas State Fair is. With the fair starting today, I thought it would be appropriate to make a few random phone calls to ask various people from all walks of life to give me their opinion of the fair, as great extravaganzas go:

Ivana Trump, former Olympian and Donald's wife – "I love the Kansas State Fair! That's why I never miss it! It just makes me so mad they shut down and always make me leave the grounds every night!"

Liza Minelli, great all-around entertainer who uses massive amounts of eye makeup – "I adore the ambience."

George Hamilton, famous permanently tanned actor – "I really look forward to the Kansas fair each year. And last year I got that exciting TV weatherman Jim O'Donnell's autograph!"

Diane von Furstenberg, socialite – "It's inspiring.

Where do they come up with all those earthy *fragrances*?"

Prince Ranier, Monaco – "I love it! I wish our country had a Kansas State Fair, but I'm afraid we're just too small."

Bianca Jagger, famous ex-wife – "It's super! I'm just so honored and flattered they even let me in every year! What? Oh, just *anybody* can get in? No matter! What I love most about the fair is the free shopping bags they hand out at The Eagle booth! Ooooh!"

Fran Lebowitz, droll but harmless New Yorker – "I like the laser-like repartee that I exchange with the witty people in the game booths. They always have entertaining tattoos, too."

Yves St. Laurent, fashion person – "The main reason I attend the Kansas State Fair each year is to see what Kansans are *wearing*. One must keep up, you know."

Ted Turner, owner of a lot of America – "Like it? Why, I love the Kansas State Fair so much I've tried repeatedly to buy it. In fact, what I'd like to do is buy it, have several duplicates made and give my wife and all my friends one. They're really amusing."

Mick Jagger, perpetual rock star – "I never miss it. That's because I like '50s music and '40s comedians."

Yoko Ono, incorrigibly famous artist – "I like to go and stand and meditate on the pinwheels in the souvenir booths."

Princess Di – "They're super! I only wish I could go much more often, but you know how Charles is."

There. Convinced, now?

See you there. (P.S. Dress is still casual.)

Even in Dodge City, "The Sun Also Rises"

December 16, 1983

News item – Dodge City plans to have Portuguese-style bullfights July 4 for the 100th anniversary of the only other bullfight ever held in Kansas.

Chapter I

"I am going to the Kansas bullfights," Jake Barnes said.

"Swell," Bill Gorton said. "Want company?"

"Sure. I will be an adviser for the bullfights. And I am going to invite Brett and Mike and Robert Cohn. We can have a reunion in Dodge City. It will be just like the old days in Spain."

"For better or worse," Bill said.

"What if you and I go to the south of Kansas to do some fishing first?"

"I have to confess, Jake, I hate fishing."

Jake stared at Bill Gorton a long time. Jake's face was very red.

"You hate to fish? You do not like to take the wine and cheese and go fish in the streams like a man?"

"No."

"Do you still like girls?"

"Knock it off, Jake."

"How many lions have you killed this year?"

"None, Jake."

"How many rhinos?"

"None – but I kicked my dog last month. And it's pretty big."

"Have you been in a plane crash yet this year? And did you enjoy it?"

"I still have more shrapnel in my leg than you do!"

"Darn! I forgot. You're a man, all right, Bill."

Chapter II

Dodge City was very hot in July 1984. It was 103 degrees the day everyone met in the Dodge LaCucaracha Motel.

"Let's find a bar and have some wine," Jake said.

The first 11 places they went sold only beer. The next nine places were private clubs and would not serve them at all.

"It was never like this in Pamplona," Mike Campbell said.

"It wasn't this bad during Prohibition!" Lady Brett said.

They bought wine in a liquor store and took it back to Jake's motel room where they talked about old times and watched TV game shows.

"How's your *aficion* holding up, Jake?" Mike asked.

"The greatest. I have 793 bullfight posters now."

Robert Cohn shook his head with awe.

Chapter III

The next day was the running of the bulls down Wyatt Earp Boulevard. The bulls hung a left at 14th Avenue and ran out to the rodeo grounds. Only Bill was trampled and seriously gored.

Jake visited Bill in the hospital and said, "I envy you."

Robert Cohn came in and asked, "Where's Brett?"

"She is with a bullfighter," Jake said.

"Pedro Romero again?"

"No. Some guy named Filbert. He is old and ugly and looks very funny in tight pants."

"What does she see in him?"

"He has a club membership."

Chapter IV

It was time for the bullfights. A bull trotted into the rodeo arena to the sound of a four-piece country and western band playing "Stand by Your Man."

Then a boy in a high school band uniform came out with a piccolo.

Jake, being an adviser, yelled to the officials, "I said you needed a p*icador*, not a piccolo!"

Filbert, the matador, appeared. He had a sword, red cape and cowboy hat.

The bull wandered up to him and sniffed his boots. Drawing his sword, Filbert yelled, "En guarde!" and started fencing with the bull's horns. Nearby, two rodeo clowns turned somersaults.

Jake roared, "Put the sword away! You're supposed to *fight* with the cape! Not *wear it!*"

Filbert was taking off the cape when a rider came charging out on a horse, roped the bull, yanked it down and tied its feet. Filbert looked at Jake, shrugged, and started hitting the bull with the cape.

"Ole," mumbled Jake.

"Wa-hoooo!" roared the crowd. "Yippeee!"

"They weren't joking about having bullfights in Kansas, were they?" Brett said.

"No," Jake said, grinning. "But isn't it pretty to think so?"

Welcome to the 20th Century, Kansas!

July 1, 1987

If there's one thing I like better than a Saturday night, it's a nice historic occasion.

A moon-landing. Hank Aaron's 715th home run. The devil personally assaulting a sleeping faith-healer. That sort of thing.

Today, of course, is an almost exceedingly historic occasion in Kansas. Effective now, July 1, 1987, after all those semidry years, 36 Kansas counties, including Sedgwick, have liquor by the drink.

What I thought I might do to mark this special occasion was call up all the most important celebrities in the world and get their personal reactions to our nice new law.

However, being a modest, one-man operation down here at the bottom of the page, I'm afraid I have neither the time nor the resources to call and chat with all the most important celebrities in the world.

But I was able to do the next-best thing. Make up some reactions that seem exactly like what some of the most important people in the world might say.

So, without further ado, here are the important made-up comments of some of the world's leading celebrities to the question: *How do you feel about Kansas' finally getting liquor by the drink?*

President Ronald Reagan – "Kansas? Kansas? Well, I think I used to broadcast baseball games on the radio in Kansas. Or maybe that was Nebraska. And maybe it was football, not baseball. Unless it was Iowa. No matter, they're, they're . . . what was the question again, Dave?"

Shirley MacLaine – "How nice. But are you sure Kansas just now got liquor by the drink? I'd swear I had a nice drink there in one of my previous lives!"

Tammy Faye Bakker – "Drinking is evil, and it is also bad for your looks. You just tell all those nice Kansans to quit drinking, and when they feel the urge to take a little nip, what they should do instead is go into their bedrooms and put on some more makeup. That will make them feel much better. Especially the third or fourth coat of all-weather, exterior, heavy-duty rouge!"

Ted Koppel – "I think some of the more forward-thinking, progressive Kansans will find the 20th century very much to their liking, Bob. And, better late than never, I always say. Welcome to the 20th century, Kansas!"

Joan Rivers – "Really? Kansas just now got liquor by the drink? Does that mean people didn't drink much before and actually used to live in Kansas when they were sober? Oh, pleeeeease."

Bruce Willis – "Hey, that's great! Wooo! So is Kansas celebrating? Having a special no-holds-barred, everything-goes party? Am I invited? When's it begin? July first? Just remember: I have to be back at work first thing in September. But I'll only come on one condition. That I am adopted as Kansas' official state party animal!"

Mr. T – "Hey, fool, don't bother me! Did you know I was gonna buy Kansas one time to wear as a necklace? It fit OK. But it wasn't shiny enough. And when I tried it on, the wheat tickled my chest."

Brian DePalma, thriller-maker – "That's nice. Say, do you think Kansas' struggle over the liquor issue would make a good movie? Were there, by any chance, any scantily dressed women and chain saws involved in the controversy?"

Leon Spinks, boxer – "Huh? You have *what* now? Liquor by the drink? That's nice – I guess. Drinking is one of the best ways to consume liquor. But, uh, how'd you do it before it was legal to consume it by drinking? Through intravenous injections? By freezing it and licking it down? Didn't you have bottles out there in Kansas or what?"

Garrison Keillor – "I'll bet Kansas is a nice state to be shy in, isn't it?"

Mikhail Gorbachev – "You got vodka in Kansas? That's nice. You sound like nice people, you Kansans. I tell you what. I make up nice little poem just for you. Ready? 'You're so nice, Kansas, that if worst comes to worst, we'll give you a break and not blow you up first!' Ja! Ja! Ja!"

Dean Martin – "Cheers, Kansas! *Twentieth-century style!*"

———

Thoughts I Couldn't Put a Stop to . . .

What do you call my fear of Carol Channing's eyes, teeth and voice? Channingophobia? Seeing her always kind of alarms me. I get this strange sensation she might sunny-disposition me to death.

•

Sure conversation stopper: "Do you know I've read the complete works of Shirley MacLaine?"

•

Has anybody with a car phone ever received a wrong-number call? An obscene phone call? A phone solicitation? Or had to say: "I'm sorry. I'll have to call you back. I'm in a car wash."

•

Ever wonder what too much MTV would do to laboratory rats?

•

Best argument that Elvis Presley is really dead and didn't just fake his death to run away and gain some privacy: If you were a famous, wealthy person and were going to stage a phony death and you had at least a shred of dignity, would you set it up so it looked as though you died constipated, reading a book on the john?

•

I like "60 Minutes" because it always has so much social and intellectual substance and Diane Sawyer sometimes wears miniskirts.

•

Someone said the average person makes 14 mistakes a day. Getting out of bed probably is always the first for many of us.

PLEASE
DON'T QUIT,
SANTA

"Labor Day. It sounds like the kind of holiday where families are supposed to get together, sit around and sweat."

1984

How to Tell if It's Love

February 13, 1987

Tomorrow being Valentine's Day, I thought it might be nice today if I batted out the definitive article about love.

Why not? Then if there's anybody who lacks great expertise in the sometimes challenging areas of love and romance, he can simply clip out this column, carry it with him at all times, and consult it in case of emergencies, especially when going barhopping or cruising.

Of course, being a serious and scholarly journalist, I didn't want to write something as important as this off the top of my head. That's why I did some research first, using an actual reference book.

To get right to the bottom of this matter, I sought the real meaning of love, and then went even further, looking for methods or tricks for distinguishing between true love and true infatuation.

I figured that distinction might come in especially handy for teenagers, since they tend to think it's possible to fall deeply and truly in love with all their hearts and souls forever about 15 times a minute.

So, here's what true love means. You might want to underline this:

"Love – A deep and tender feeling of affection for or attachment or devotion to a person or persons." (From Webster's New World Dictionary . . . nobody ever said Webster was a poet. You want your meanings of love to rhyme or something, try Byron or Shelley.)

Now, I suppose some of you are saying, "OK, Bob.

130

That's nice to know. But how can I tell whether my deep and tender feelings of affection for or attachment or devotion to someone, like the gorgeous chick across the aisle in Chemistry, are the real thing or mere, common infatuation?"

That's a good question, and a challenging one. I had to flip all the way back to the letter "i" before I came up with the answer:

"Infatuated – Completely carried away by foolish shallow love or affection." (Ibid.)

Got that straight? No? Then let me give you an example.

Infatuation is when you think you are madly, deeply and head-over-heels in love with someone, and you want to drop out of the 10th grade and marry him tomorrow, even though there are still some things you don't know about the boy, such as his name, what kind of car he drives, and how much his allowance is.

Love, on the other hand, is a deep, abiding, beautiful, meaningful experience built on important mutual values and interests, such as, say, you are a Libra and she is an Aries, you both are just wild about Cyndi Lauper, Tom Cruise, pepperoni pizza and bowling, and your relationship has withstood the test of time, having endured a whole month.

OK. Now that we've got the true meaning of love out of the way, so you won't go and do something really dumb that you'll regret for the rest of your life, like go on an expensive Caribbean cruise with the wrong person, here's a little test for you.

Get some of these right, and I have a feeling you've heard about this thing called love before, you mature, sophisticated smoothie, you.

1. What is love? (a) Never having to say you're sorry (Ali MacGraw). (b) blue. (c) metaphysical gravity (Buckminster Fuller) (d) other.

2. Why is it generally accepted that Romeo and Juliet

were really in love? (a) Faith in Shakespeare. (b) He didn't drive a Trans Am, she didn't wear designer jeans, she didn't talk like a Valley Girl and he didn't wear untied Reeboks, but they still admired each other.

3. Who was St. Valentine? (a) Founded Hallmark card company. (b) Founded Whitman candy company. (c) Nobody is sure he existed. (d) The first really prosperous flower salesman. (e) The greatest saint of them all, being the guy who invented love, romance and hanky-panky.

4. Why is Valentine's Day on Feb. 14? (a) That's the day the first love song was written. (b) That's the day when, the story goes, birds begin to pair off. (c) That's the day Adam got up the nerve to ask Eve out on their first date.

ANSWERS (in alphabetical order): a, b, c, d.

Valentines You Won't Find in Stores

February 14, 1990

Does anybody else have as much trouble as I do picking out greetings cards for special occasions?

If you do, I ought to send you a sympathy card, but I won't, because it's just too much trouble.

I hate picking out cards.

They're never exactly right.

No matter how appropriate a card may be, there's almost always one word or one phrase or something that doesn't quite apply to the person you're getting the card for.

For instance, if the message inside a card expresses your love and passion almost perfectly, the words on the outside will say something inappropriate or dumb like, "To a valued customer."

Or if the words and art on the outside are perfect, maybe saying, "To whom it may concern," or "To the world's greatest human being," the message on the inside will be all wrong, expressing sentiments like, "Congratulations on your new garden tractor from the gang at the office!"

Maybe I take picking out cards too seriously. It takes me longer, sometimes, to find just the right card for people than it takes other earthlings to buy a new car.

I wonder whether others are as picky as I am.

What if, say, you always call your boyfriend or girl-friend "sweetheart," but a card you like says, "For You, Honey!" Would you get the card, anyway?

I wouldn't.

When I get a card, I don't want one false note on it.

A card may say exactly how I feel about someone, but if it has one extra little false observation, like, " . . . and I love the way you wiggle your ears when you smile adoringly at me," I want no part of it.

Of course, you can always buy those cards that are blank inside with very romantic scenes on the outside of the silhouettes of two young people walking along the beach at sunset with their pants cuffs rolled up, but sometimes those cards just don't seem right somehow, especially when you live 1,500 miles from the nearest serious beach.

When I think about all the different, complicated kinds of relationships there are, I think the card industry could do a lot better.

How about Valentines like these?

To My Long-suffering Spouse
Our marriage isn't what it used to be,
And we may not be in love anymore,

But here's a card and some candy, spouse;
That's what the day is for.

Or . . .

A Card for You, Son
Well, son, it's Valentine's Day
So I'll give you this card and poem,
Expressing my surprise once again
You still haven't run away from home!

To My Steady, Reliable Friend
We may not be that happy,
We may not have much to say,
But until one of us can do better
I guess what we have is OK.

To My Much-Appreciated Spouse
On a scale of one to 10
I still love you more than 3,
But what I really love, my dear,
Is your six-figure salary!

A Valentine From Your Local Newspaper
Do you know how much we love you?
Do you know how much we care?
Do you know how much our price went up?
Hello? Hello? Are you still there?

How to Make
Labor Day *Work*

September 5, 1988

Labor Day.

Whoopee, etc., right?

Labor Day.

Does anybody ever really think about Labor Day?

Is the unexamined holiday worth celebrating? Worth anything?

I tried to ponder Labor Day one year, but it was too much like hard work so I quit. But maybe the time has come today to try again.

Labor Day is the one serious holiday that nobody rhapsodizes about or waxes poetic over or goes to church to observe. Some might, however, wax churches that day.

Labor Day is the no-frills holiday.

It has no gimmicks, no tradition, no cherished old customs, no power steering, no air conditioning, no AM-FM radio.

Nobody sends Labor Day cards out.

There is no Labor Day bunny, no traditional Labor Day turkey, no Labor Day tree to put up and trim, no nice, bright, Labor Day decorations, no football bowl games to watch all day and night on television, no Labor Day fireworks display.

It doesn't even sound good – Labor Day.

Labor Day sounds like the kind of day you'd dread, not look forward to as a day off.

It sounds oppressive, demanding, like a special day when you ought to do some significant labor for once in your life, such as take the engine out of your car and put it

135

back in just for the work of it.

Labor Day. It sounds like the kind of holiday where families are supposed to get together, sit around and sweat.

It sounds like the kind of day that always ought to fall on a weekend, with the proper way of observing it being to work.

That is, businesses that are ordinarily closed on, say, Sundays, would hang out signs the preceding week and run ads such as:

Kansas State Bank & Trust will be open all day Sunday in observance of Labor Day.

City Hall will be open from 9 to 5 Sunday for Labor Day.

Attention, parents of students: Your children will be expected to attend classes Sunday from 9 a.m. to noon to observe Labor Day.

Dear subscribers: Because your faithful, ever-vigilant newspaper, The Eagle, never takes a day off, it will observe Labor Day this year by putting out two papers instead of one.

Things like that.

Labor Day simply doesn't sound like fun and games, it sounds like sweat and grunting and sore muscles and blisters.

It would seem to conjure up all the joyous holiday spirit of grease under the fingernails, blasting alarm clocks, heavy work shoes, hard hats, jackhammers and smoke billowing out of factories.

Labor Day sounds blue-collar. That's because you really can't think of most white-collar work as actual labor.

I know I could never bring myself to say that what I am doing at this very moment is labor.

What I do, writing words for a living, may be work and it may even be hard work in its strange way, but tapping typewriter keys is not what some people would call major manual labor, no matter how sticky and hard my "W" and "K" keys may be to thump down.

I wonder, if Labor Day were upgraded into more of a traditional holiday, what kind of Labor Day card would we send out to people? A Social Security greeting card?

What Labor Day songs could we sing?

"Nine to Five"? "Hard Day's Night"?

No doubt the traditional Labor Day holiday meal would be beer, beef jerkies and pretzels.

This is a holiday I love, though. There's no pressure. You don't feel obligated to have a good time, and you don't feel disappointed if you don't have one.

And for those of us who think we should actually do something special on Labor Day to observe the great American tradition of hard work, we can always do something that is more difficult to endure and more strenuous and painful than the most physically demanding jobs.

Watch Jerry Lewis.

———

For the Man or Woman Who Has Everything . . .

November 4, 1985

Already the season's first disgusting catalog advertising exotic (as in decadent and expensive) Christmas gifts has arrived on my desk.

These annoying catalogs are so vulgar they're enough to make anybody with any taste turn right to the Yellow Pages to look for a monastery to join.

In fact, assuming everybody else is as appalled as I am

by these catalogs, I've been thinking of doing everyone a favor and opening my own, conveniently located refuge for everybody who wants to get away from all the grubby, money-hungry hustlers out there. I'm thinking of calling it Bob's Monastery, Convent & Pizzeria. Membership fees would be reasonable, with special family rates.

It's just that the hucksters who put out these catalogs are giving decadence a bad name.

Imagine paying $75 for an Abercrombie & Fitch rubber-band shooting gun, when you could go out and get something equally neat and novel like a cigarette lighter shaped like an attractive nubile person for just – what? – $4.99?

It just drives me crazy seeing exotic gifts like hair dryers you can use underwater, not because they aren't practical necessities, but because they're always overpriced, like $60,000, or at least $950.

What the world needs is an outlet that offers exotic Christmas gifts that the average person can afford but that are still so nifty we can send them to our brother-in-law and people like that and show them how clever we are without having to go bankrupt to prove it.

What the world needs is something like this:

THE AVERAGE JOE & JANE'S EXOTIC BUT AFFORDABLE XMAS CATALOG

A. Polyester jelly beans. Available in red, green, black, orange, white or mixed. They make no sense at all but are terrific conversation pieces, and visitors will probably think they came from Neiman Marcus and are very chic and expensive. $6.99 lb. (WARNING: Non-edible.)

B. High-heeled, furry-lined house slippers. $4.99. One size fits all. (Stretchable).

C. Chocolate wristbands. For exercise nuts who don't need to lose weight. $1.25 pr.

D. Leopard-design car "clothes." Tired of seeing your car the same old color? Dress it in a customized, washable, leopard-skin cover that slips snugly over all kinds of cars and fits better than you'd think, with slits for windows, doors, tires and lights. Comes in S, M, L, XL. $49.99. (Guaranteed 99 percent shrink-proof.)

E. Authentic Xeroxed copies of a Nancy Sinatra record album cover with phony autograph that probably looks just like her handwriting. $1.99 ea. Or $2 a doz.

F. Realistic false dimples. They'll make you irresistible. When you want to smile winningly, simply cover your mouth as though yawning and stick on. Looks a lot like actual sexy hollows in cheeks. $1.99 a pair. $2.99 for executive, waterproof model.

G. Tiny alligator patches. Sew on shirts, sweaters, jackets, shoes, car covers, children's foreheads. $5 a lb.

H. Phony oil wells. Impress your friends and neighbors and mother-in-law. Looks exactly like the real thing, except up close. $39.99. Or six for $150.

I. Red-velvet tennis ball covers. For the real tennis aficionado. Really impress the people on adjacent courts by protecting your tennis balls while you play with these beautiful, smooth covers that fit like a glove on regulation tennis balls. Ideal for players who prefer slower surfaces. 3 for $19.99. Dry-clean only.

J. Beautiful views. Attractive pictures of scenery to stick on windows at home, especially in southeastern and south-central Kansas. Check one or more: Waikiki Beach. A tree with a little bird in it. Rocky Mountains. Swiss Alps. Derby city park. Loni Anderson. Christmas in Vermont. An Eastborough back yard. Part of the Eiffel Tower. Dallas Cowboys cheerleaders. $4.99 for small windows. $39.99 for picture windows. $1 discounts on reprints ordered later.

139

Please send cash only and allow six weeks to 60 years for delivery.

What if We Have to Replace Santa?

December 24, 1986

I don't want to alarm you the day before Christmas, boys and girls, but have you given much thought to the possibility Santa Claus might retire?

Now, relax. No need to bawl. Nothing is imminent, as far as I know. Just dry those tears. But Santa's no spring chicken, you know.

So it could get very interesting if he called it quits, took his golf clubs and retired to a fancy condo in St. Petersburg.

Who would fill the vacancy?

Not to worry. My guess is everybody would want to replace him. To become the new Santa Claus. Because if you're Santa, you're your own boss, you're beloved, you're respected.

So just imagine, kiddies, what kind of job various people would do if they were chosen to take over as the new Santa Claus. . . .

Governor Haydenclaus – As soon as he takes over, he cuts back on everybody's gifts 3.8 percent across the board.

David Lettermanclaus – Instead of giving people gifts for Christmas, he goes around the world playing practical jokes on them, waking them up in the middle of the night to get them to watch him do something dumb and, all the while, a network's TV camera films it all so everybody gets humiliated on national television.

Bob Stephanclaus – He even refuses to say "Ho ho ho," referring all children who want to talk to him to his attorney.

Jim Bakkerclaus – With Bakkerclaus, everybody gets the same thing for Christmas every year. An LP of Tammy singing Christmas carols.

Gloria Steinemclaus – All good little boys get dollies, and all good little girls get footballs.

Frank Sinatraclaus – A generous Santa, if ever there was one. Except he sues everybody who has ever written any unauthorized Christmas poems or songs about him, and he wants to punch out the guy who called him a "jolly old elf."

Hugh Hefnerclaus – Replaces elves with more luscious little helpers at the North Pole. But they all, not being allowed to wear enough clothes, freeze to death.

Cosby Claus – Very popular with the kids. Except his repeated, extended cutesy monologues finally drive the reindeer nuts.

Larry Brownclaus – Four hours after he replaces Santa, the New York Post reports he is considering changing jobs and taking over for the Easter Bunny.

Bruce Springsteenclaus – He develops a small cult following early, but it takes him 10 years to really catch on.

Ron Reagan Juniorclaus – "I'll try anything once," he explains. "Except work."

Chuck Yeagerclaus (aka Mr. Right Stuffclaus) – Sets new Christmas speed record but only four reindeer survive the pace, and Rudolph's nose suffers burnout.

John McEnroeclaus – Argues with elves. Argues with reindeer. Gets the job done, magnificently. But he offends and alienates so many people nobody wants to sit on his lap or leave him cookies.

Nicholas Daniloffclaus – Gets arrested for spying the

first time he goes down a chimney in the Soviet Union.

Oral Robertsclaus – All the kiddies who send him letters saying what they want for Christmas get on his mailing list, and Oral sends them emotional, frightening form letters back, saying if they don't send him $50, he won't be able to make his trip, come Christmas.

Joan Riversclaus – After two tedious weeks of Riversclaus and department store Riversclauses, kids are so turned off that Christmas is canceled, and everybody is relieved and grateful.

Bob Hopeclaus – Hopeclaus doesn't just take gifts along on his Christmas trips, he also takes Brooke Shields, Anita Bryant, Anita Ekberg, the Associated Press' current All-America football team and Miss 1987 Artichoke Festival, and then his trips are televised later as TV specials that all look and sound alike.

Santa Reagan – People love him. But on his very first Christmas trip, he gets hopelessly lost and just flies around and around for eight years, trying to figure out where he's at, where he's going and what he's supposed to do with the reins.

———

Saying Thank You Isn't Always Easy

December 23, 1984

I never used to be much good at Christmases when I was a little kid.

What pressure.

I always felt like I was letting everybody down when I opened my presents from them on Christmas mornings.

142

I never felt as though I acted excited and grateful enough – especially when I'd unwrap a basketball-shaped bar of funny-colored bath soap with a rope on it so you could hang it around your neck.

I worried I'd spoil my parents' Christmases when I opened presents because I never acted the way little kids did on TV and in the movies.

On TV and in the movies, little blond-haired, sunny-faced kids (sometimes with freckles) never acted like me when they opened gifts on Christmas and other gainful occasions.

Whenever their moms and dads gave these demented little twerps presents, they would open them breathlessly (movie presents just open by lifting the tops off), and express more emotion in 15 seconds than Olivier did in his whole career.

Joy, oh, joy! These cute, little movie cherubs would yelp and shout, their faces glowing with rapture, "Thanks, Mom! Thanks, Dad!" and run and give both parents great, big, warm hugs and kisses, and the three of them would just stay like that awhile, hugging and smiling and stuff, especially after Billy discovered he got the shiny red fire engine.

For a long time I figured that's the way I was supposed to act, too, every time I opened a gift that wasn't underwear. I was really a dummy. I also figured movies showed the way all my friends probably acted in the privacy of their homes. But I still couldn't do it.

I'd just smile the best I could and say thanks. It wasn't that I was ungrateful and unappreciative. I just never was much for lovey-dovey stuff.

Showing your feelings and all.

Maybe it had to do with the role models I looked up to – my grandfather, my father and Dracula. And even now – what can I say? – I'll take them over Phil Donahue and Alan

Alda. I can't help it. I'm voluntarily hopeless.

But I did worry when I was a kid about hurting my mother's feelings, in particular, because I never acted giddy like TV kids.

Even if on a Christmas morning someone had given me the gift of my dreams, the entire Cleveland Indians baseball franchise, I would have just smiled and said, "Hey, thanks! This is really nice."

Being giddy has always been difficult for me, even the year I was 11.

There I was, sitting on the floor, greedily ripping open another package and, wow, there was a new Chico Carrasquel baseball glove! The card said, From Mom.

I was beside myself. There was a God! And I couldn't wait till spring.

Nothing, you see, meant as much to me as a baseball glove, mainly because nothing in life meant more to me than playing baseball – nothing I would admit, anyway. I mean, there was Rita Kay.

But, hey. Even though Rita Kay was by far the most lovely and awe-inspiring femme fatale in our entire grade school, heck, if you came right down to it and got your priorities straight, what good was she when somebody smacked a hot line drive your way at shortstop?

Yet even when I got that cherished glove, looked up at my mother over in her chair and thanked her the best I could manage, I felt like I didn't sound genuinely grateful and appreciative, really letting her know how much the glove meant to me.

Maybe she thought, "I wonder if he would have liked another bar of soap with a rope on it better."

Christmas has always been my mother's favorite time of the year. Six years ago, when she was 56, doctors gave her about two years to live. But she's still hanging in there, fighting, back in Indiana. She knows each Christmas might be her last.

I just wonder yet if she used to know, especially the years after she had to finish raising my brother, sister and me alone, how much I appreciated the Christmases, and the gifts, she gave us.

Even – in fact, especially – the bars of soap with rope on them.

———

Thoughts I Couldn't Put a Stop to . . .

Ever get up in the morning, yawn, stretch and thank God because you're an American, free, have a roof over your head, a little food to eat and you're not Geraldo Rivera?

•

People who actually know the words to heavy metal songs make me nervous.

•

Has any name ever been more awesome than Simone de Beauvoir?

•

Joke making the rounds: The sun is supposed to burn out in 16 billion years. Do you know what that means? The work on West Kellogg in Wichita will have to be finished in complete darkness.

•

Do you ever wonder if you look as silly when you dance as so many other people do?

MIND IF I GET PERSONAL?

"Don't let a little midlife crisis spoil your whole evening."

1985

Which to Have?
Kids or a Dog?

April 3, 1978

My wife and I are dogless. So far.

After six years of marriage, we still have no dog – nor any other kind of pet, for that matter.

That's the way I like it, and I'm not ashamed of being dogless, no matter what people may say.

The truth is that we don't have a dog by choice, and I'm responsible for the choice.

When my wife and I first considered marriage, we discussed all those important things that have to do with a couple's being compatible.

We discussed how each of us thinks a toothpaste tube should be squeezed (from the bottom so you can fold it up or from just anywhere?).

We discussed our preferences for TV shows. "If a good comedy conflicted with a good drama," we asked each other, "which would you want to watch?" We agreed that it was unlikely that there would ever be two good shows on TV in any one season, let alone on the same night.

We discussed our philosophies about putting your feet up on the coffee table. We agreed that it was ridiculous to let this issue stand in the way of our marriage when we probably wouldn't be able to afford furniture for five years.

We discussed dogs.

I have nothing personal against dogs. It's animals in general that I object to – in the house. What are zoos for, anyway? Should I ever feel the need for the companionship of a bird or beast, I'll go visit a giraffe.

I told my wife that I liked other people's dogs just fine – as long as they didn't try to bite, lick or chew me, but I just wasn't cut out to have a dog of my own.

She said she'd love to have a dog but would rather have children. How did I feel about having kids?

That threw me. Did she mean that if I didn't want kids, then she'd insist upon getting a dog? Before answering, I sneaked off to decide whether I preferred kids to dogs.

Dogs shed hair on the sofa, I thought. Kids don't. Score one for a kid.

Dogs have to be housebroken. Kids have to be toilet-trained. Those facts canceled each other out.

When you house-train dogs, you don't have to buy them diapers. For kids, you do. Score one for a dog.

Dogs chew up your socks. Kids try to flush your socks down the toilet. Those canceled out.

When a dog has to go outside, you have to get up and open the door for him twice. A kid could open the door himself, so you could keep watching the ball game, uninterrupted. Kid 2, dog 1.

Dogs can be watchdogs. Kids can't. You can't give a kid a gun and have him sleep on the floor by the door. Kid 2, dog 2.

Kids cost a lot of money and go to college. Dogs bite people and get you sued for everything you've got. Kid 3, dog 2.

In the end, I decided I'd prefer kids to a dog. The score of my decision was a one-sided 87-66.

So now we have three kids. And now I find out I forgot to consider one major thing when I was making my decision.

When a kid gets old enough, as our son has, he begs and begs for a dog. A dog does not beg you to get him a kid.

So much for well-thought-out 87-66 decisions. I'm

afraid that my dogless days are numbered and that there are dog days ahead.

———

Pushy? Who?
This Little League Dad?

June 13, 1982

So my son's first Little League game was last week.

No big deal.

Kids crawl for the first time. Walk for the first time. Talk. Get measles. Mumps. Start school. Join Little League. Get arrested for armed robbery. There's always a first time for everything. Right?

You take a snapshot, life goes on.

Little League is just a stage that adults – I mean, kids – go through. Like the Terrible Twos and pimples. Right?

Chase is 9. The reason he didn't join sooner was because I didn't want to push him. Never mind that by the time last summer we found out how to get him in, the season was almost over.

Whatever. Pushing your kid into sports can be unhealthy. A kid should play games to have fun, not so Dad can get some vicarious jollies.

No way would I want to be a father who drives his son relentlessly, pushing, criticizing, overemphasizing sports.

Who knows what that would do to the delicate psyche of an impressionable child?

They'd probably become twisted and warped.

Grow up to sign a big-league contract. Become another Pete Rose, obsessed with getting his uniform dirty and sweating more than anybody else to prove his worth as a human being. Never read a book. Never draw a picture. Never read anything in the newspaper except sports. Overdevelop his competitiveness to the extent that on nights when the moon is full, his ears will grow pointed, hair will sprout from his forehead and he'll turn into another Billy Martin or Attila the Hun. Or worse, he might start chewing . . . tobacco!

Anyway, Chase's first game was Wednesday evening.

I decided I'd go. What the heck.

Big difference, you know, between being pushy and being supportive.

I drove us all to the game. Got home from work two hours earlier than necessary. A boy doesn't want to be late for his first Little League game, after all.

Chase was ready. In his gray uniform, green cap and socks. Number 11. Pete Rose should look so athletic.

At the ballpark while Chase warmed up, I figured out a little trick to avoid boredom before my only son's first official organized baseball game ever. I watched his every move.

Chase's first official at-bat came in the second inning, his team, the swift and powerful Raiders, already leading, 4-1.

Sitting with my wife on the hood of our car, I pounded the hood supportively with the heels of my hands and observed, "This could be rather interesting."

Then I advised, "Just meet the ball, Chase! And knock it into Oklahoma!"

After a couple of impressive foul balls a few feet in the direction of first base, Chase drew a walk.

"See? Look at that! A walk! Babe Ruth walked a lot. Maybe we have a little Babe Ruth on our hands!"

Mac, who is a great young player, smashed a hit into right center. Chase was off, running, rounding third, heading for home.

151

"Slide!" I coached, helpfully. "Spike him! Rip the catcher's ankles off!"

"You yell things like that, you'll not only humiliate me," my wife said, "but you'll get arrested."

Chase scored standing up. And beaming.

After three innings, it was 16-7, Raiders. But in the top of the fifth and final innning, the Dunkin Donuts Royals got a rally rolling. It was 16-10 . . . 16-11 . . . 16-12 . . .

"Kill the ump!" I admonished, supportively. "Fire the coach! Don't let this game slip away! Stomp on 'em!"

. . . 16-13 . . . 16-14 . . . 16-15 . . . and then the third out was made, and the game was over. Raiders 16, Royals 15. Chase had walked twice, scored twice.

"What'd you think?" Lisa asked.

"Oh, it was sort of interesting, I guess," I said. "I might even give some thought to coming to the next game. Only one thing bothers me, though."

"What's that?"

"I'm not sure I saw any big-league scouts here."

Who Says Father Knows Best?

June 16, 1985

I always knew I wasn't good father material.

All I had to do was think about what the world's greatest TV fathers were like in action, and it was obvious I wasn't cut out to be a Hall-of-Fame-caliber patriarch.

These TV dads were so perfect that they almost made

152

such virtues as patience, kindness and wisdom nauseating and depressing.

You know who I mean: Ozzie Nelson. Jim Anderson. Ward Cleaver. Ben Cartwright. Gomez Addams.

All those dads were relentlessly pleasant, almost to a fault, except occasionally when Ben Cartwright would have to shoot somebody.

Ozzie Nelson was so easygoing that I think if David and Ricky had robbed a bank, hijacked a plane, joined a devil-worshiping cult and even started wearing earrings, ole Ozzie would have just chuckled tolerantly and observed, "Boys will be boys."

Jim ("Father Knows Best") Anderson not only never got mad like I do, I don't think he even frowned. Maybe he drank decaffeinated coffee.

The TV father I remember most fondly is Gomez Addams of "The Addams Family." He wasn't obtrusively nice or even conspicuously wise. He always kind of acted like he'd just got off the bus from Saturn, was amused, but a little befuddled, by everything and wasn't quite sure he wanted to stay. That's a pretty good perspective, if you ask me.

But now that I'm thinking about it, I realize the way I approached fatherhood was out of character. Without reading a book.

That is, whenever I tried something new and important when I was young, I always got books to learn proper style and fundamentals.

So I read lots of classic educational books with titles like "How to Make the World Forget Sandy Koufax," "How to Hit the Ball 500 Feet Every Time," "Basketball Fundamentals for the Whole Family," "How to Beat Everybody to a Pulp," "How to Write Sentences Without Making a Complete Fool of Yourself," "How to Be More

Like Cary Grant Than Cary Grant," etc.

But, unbelievably, I've never read a single book along the lines of "How to Be a Wise Father Without Making Your Kids Hate You."

And now Chase is 12, and Page and Tracy are 9 already.

They're zipping right along growing up, and here I am, still trying to figure out what you're supposed to do when you're the father in the house.

It hasn't been easy. I remember when Chase was born. With all the words he had to learn, I worried about whether there was something special fathers were supposed to do so their babies could learn to talk.

I wondered whether I should chant words over and over like, "Crib. Diaper. Toy. Happy. Wet. Draconian. Obfuscation."

It's amazing how kids start spouting sentences on their own.

But what's always troubled me most about not being good father material is the sad fact that I'm not always tapping my kids on the shoulder and wowing them with words of wisdom.

I mean, I believe yet that good fathers everywhere sit down in their favorite chairs at least twice a week, puff on a pipe, and then when their devoted children gather eagerly around, these dads share all sorts of wisdom and pithy sayings while the kids listen with reverence and awe, interrupting only to applaud especially brilliant insights.

I never do that.

When my kids grow up, they'll never tell anybody, "Well, it's like my dad used to say. . . . "

It's pathetic. I even knew a sportswriter once who raised his two kids by Shakespeare's words, "To thine own self be true."

Me, I don't know what to say. A guru I'm not.

Maybe I could tell my kids what Ring Lardner told his sons:

"Don't ever kill yourself. You don't know why you've been put here, but there's probably a reason and you should fulfill it."

But I find that fatherly gem a little flat and depressing.

Heck. I can't even remember what Gomez Addams told his kids.

Probably, "Don't forget to feed the spider."

Thank God my kids got their mother.

———

Are Dads Better or Worse Today?

June 17, 1990

Fathers aren't what they used to be.

Anybody else ever notice?

Fathers are just nothing like they used to be back when I was a goofy, impressionable little kid in the '50s, and maybe we middle-age dads today should be ashamed of ourselves.

I am convinced, after thinking about this matter very intensely over a couple of especially inspirational martinis last night, that our fathers acted a lot more like grown-ups than we fathers do today.

Nowadays, dads are more like aging kids than grown-ups.

As I remember, there seemed to be something much more serious, substantial and dignified about fathers back then.

Fathers didn't act like kids in those days. They didn't dress silly, and they didn't go out and play the way we do all the time now.

Some fathers, in fact, didn't even want their *kids* to act like kids in those days, that's how serious, substantial and dignified those dads were.

I had a relative, Uncle Gustaf P. Getz, who always worried ferociously that his kids were going to be roasted in hell forever if he ever failed to provide them with "chores" to do every waking second of every single day save Sunday.

Times have changed. Dads have changed.

I think I know why.

Our dads grew up during hard times. They lived through the Depression.

They all had to get up at dawn and touch cows and then, when they were done, walk five miles in the snow to school every day until they finally had to drop out to take a job to help support their aging parents, five brothers, three sisters and strange Aunt Tillie.

But we, today's dads, grew up watching the Mickey Mouse Club and Howdy Doody and reading comic books about cute rodents, temperamental ducks and strange heroes who wore tights, capes and masks.

No wonder we turned out so shallow and silly, right?

Our kids today probably have no idea of how restrained, dreary, substantial and grown-up previous parents used to be.

Back then, for instance . . .

Dads did not put on funny, shiny, tight pants and space helmets and go riding around in public on bicycles.

(There was one man in my hometown who rode a bike. That was weird old Mr. Chauncey, who was so addled that whenever any parents saw him come wobbling slowly up the street, they'd shoo their kids inside.)

Dads also did not wear tank tops, tennis shoes, or any other footwear that looked youthful or stylish, although in those days, no footwear looked youthful and stylish.

Almost no dads ran around in shorts, except to swim, nor did grown-up men wear jeans.

Some dads, however, like my neighbor, the skinny, little, chain-smoking Mr. Noggins, who edited the local paper, would put on stunningly sporty Bermuda shorts to mow his lawn.

But even so, Mr. Noggins, father of two, had the maturity and dignity never to get a tan, so that his legs were always a respectable, deathly white color.

Dads weren't always talking about their weight, their age and their cholesterol. Ah, those were the days.

Dads did not run up and down the streets and sidewalks committing the now-popular atrocity called jogging.

Dads always seemed to be doing something sort of important, even if it was just reading the paper, and none I knew ever did anything that could ever be called "going outside and playing." Kids did that.

So, dads are different now.

Essentially, we dads today are overly concerned with clothes, stereos, TV shows, exercising, making money and staying young forever, which, of course, is exactly the same things we were interested in when we were 14.

It's embarrassing, if you ask me.

Dads now are so much less serious than our dads, so immature, so childlike, fun-loving and silly.

I just hope our kids appreciate it.

Are You Surviving Your Teenagers?

June 16, 1991

Happy dad's day, fellow father persons. Guess what?

It's time for another gloriously revealing Father's Day test. A kind of follow-up checkup for aging, battered patriarchs.

Five years ago, I came up with an immeasurably insightful and helpful quiz for determining how well you were doing in the fathering department.

No doubt, grateful dads all over Kansas took that quiz, found out what a shamefully faulty job they were doing, sought out their wives, asked how many offspring they had, and thereupon resolved to be much better fathers, or, at the very least, get on a first-name basis with their curious little progeny and delightful little deductions.

This week, as I was rereading that test, it occurred to me that it was completely geared toward men with young kids, while today, a lot of the dads who took that quiz have teenagers on their hands, and are probably overdue, then, for a five-year checkup.

So, without further ado, here's a new, updated How Well Are You Coping With Your Teenagers, Dad? test. . . .

1. How many of your kids haven't run away from home permanently yet? (Give yourself 10 points per child.)

2. Do any of your kids still listen to you when you talk?

3. Would they, if they ever stayed home when you told them to?

4. Are your teenagers home so seldom that you have issued them name tags so you'll remember who they are on

158

the occasions they show up?

5. To find out what kind of a disciplinarian you are, what do you think is a reasonable weekday summer curfew for your teenager?

(a) 3 p.m., just to have an edge.

(b) 10 p.m.

(c) Midnight.

(d) They should be home and in bed by Aug. 20 sharp, and not a minute later! This way they should be back in time for the opening of school.

6. Could your teenagers teach Ferris Bueller some tricks?

7. Could your teenagers teach Hunter S. Thompson tricks?

8. Could your teenagers even teach Ted Kennedy some tricks?

9. How would you best describe your kids' friends?

(a) Pretty wholesome. None of them has violated his parole, anyway.

(b) Very good influences. All make it to school every day, no matter what they did the night before.

(c) High-spirited and lively. These friends would scare Hell's Angels. They're also not as well-dressed or well-groomed as Hell's Angels.

10. Does your teenager tend to stay out so late every night you probably wouldn't even notice if he or she ran away from home?

11. Does your teen ever confide in you and seek comfort from you, after, say, he or she has gone.to a party the night before and had a disturbing experience when there was no booze available?

12. Do you ever find yourself shrugging off certain things your kid does as "being a typical teenager" when that same behavior, in your day, not only would've given your parents a stroke, but would have prompted J. Edgar Hoover to name you Public Enemy No. 1?

13. Given the choice between having your teenager or Saddam Hussein live with you the next two years, is there any remote chance you'd actually pick your kid, and, if so, would you still pick him or her if Saddam promised to clean his room every month?

14. If your teenager hasn't caused you a moment's grief, please explain how you did it, what sort of lock you put on his doors, what kind of bars on his windows, etc.

15. Even if your teenager survives and grows out of this phase, what do you think the chances are that you'll ever be the same again, and no longer need the therapy and strait-jacket?

How You Scored: *If this quiz amused you, you're probably doing a fantastic job as a pop. But if you're shaking and sobbing deliriously by now, well, sorry, but just remember: Sanity is probably very overrated.*

Unhappy Birthday to You, Unhappy Birthday to You ...

October 2, 1983

• "Forty is, I observe from not too great a distance, an awkward age. It's an age at which people have histories and options. At 30, they had perhaps less history. At 50, perhaps fewer options. But at 40, it hangs in the balance. The person we thought we might be, still challenges the person we are." – Ellen Goodman, columnist, 1979.

• "Now that I'm 40 . . . I'll be asking powerful questions

like, 'What is life all about?' and 'Who am I, actually?' " –
John Leo, in a Newsweek essay, 1977.

• "The 40th is, truth be told, a boring birthday. . . . I wish
I could serve up, on a silver slaver, some glistening original
thought gleaned from 40 years' experience. But the essential
wisdom of life is deflating." – George F. Will, columnist,
April 1981.

• "Forty – sombre anniversary to the hedonist – in seek-
ers after truth like Buddha, Mahomet, Mencius, St. Ignatius,
the turning-point of their lives." – Cyril Connolly, "The
Unquiet Grave."

• "A fool at 40 is a fool indeed." – Edward Young.

• "No man is ever old enough to know better." –
Holbrook Jackson.

• "I am turning 40 this week. It's not at all that bad. It's
better than turning green, or turning sour. It's better than
turning into a beetle." – Ellen Goodman, April 1981.

•

You guessed it. I just turned 40.

Forty.

I think I'd rather turn into a beetle.

If I could be a young beetle.

But I think I can take being 40. I have no plans to throw
in the towel or hang up my spikes. I intend to remain active.
Get some fresh air every day. Sunshine. Take up a nice
hobby.

The important thing when you're getting up in years, as
I understand it, is to try to feel useful. But I'm afraid that
won't be easy. I never felt useful before.

As you can see above, I have been saving articles and
quotations the last few years about turning 40.

I wanted to have them handy so that when I turned 40, I
could reread them and know how to feel on such a historic,
monumental occasion.

161

So here I am, 40 now, but I find I don't need any help at all expressing how it feels.

Turning 40 stinks. You can quote me on that (Hear that, Bartlett's? Turning 40 stinks.).

Just think. In only 60 years, I will be 100. I don't even want to think about it.

Jonathan Swift said that no wise man ever wished to be younger.

Jonathan Swift's mind must have been muddled with old age when he said that.

He got it backward. Only an idiot wouldn't want to be younger.

You think Ponce de Leon was a dummy, maybe? What old Ponce was, was middle-aged when, probably opening his shirt another button, putting a gold chain around his neck and letting his hair grow over his collar, he went looking for the fountain of youth.

Two things you'll never hear me say (as long as I am in control of my faculties, anyway) are "You're not old – age is just a number" and "Hey, you're only as old as you feel."

Dumber words were never spoken.

Of course our age is "just" a number. So is our weight. And our house payment. And the speed limit. And a bodily temperature of 105.

No matter how good we may look or how young we may *feel*, if we're 40, we're 40, for better or worse, and not as young as we used to be.

Someone once told Gloria Steinem that she didn't look 40. She replied, "But this is the way 40 looks."

Good old Gloria . . .

It's probably sort of true, too, that at 40 we have fewer options.

I mean, I'm not going to kid myself anymore.

I think my chances of ever playing shortstop for a living

with the Cleveland Indians are getting pretty remote.

And my chances of ever winning a batting championship are probably completely out of the question.

Depressing, isn't it?

But I can tell you for a fact that there is a bright side to turning an old and feebleminded 40. And this is no joke.

I have this curious, totally unexpected feeling that I'm almost grown up now.

———

Midlife Crisis – or Coffee Nerves?

June 10, 1984

Please excuse the confusion down here at the bottom of this page today, but the resident columnist seems to be going through a rather awkward stage right now, a difficult phase.

If his thinking seems in total disarray, it's because one little thing seems to have him baffled for the moment.

Reality.

"The older you get, the more befuddling reality becomes," he said to his wife the other night.

"What now, my love?" she asked.

He showed her a magazine article he had just received unexpectedly from an old buddy.

The buddy had been a helicopter door gunner with the First Cav in the Central Highlands in Vietnam, and the article was about Delayed Stress Reaction, or Post-Traumatic Stress Disorder.

There were 24 symptoms listed, and somebody – there was no explanation for this either – had checked 18 of the 24 symptoms.

"Are you upset," his wife asked, "because this suggests that your friend is really messed up and maybe calling out for help?"

"It's not that."

"What is it then?"

"The symptoms. Look at them."

She looked. Among them, there were these:

Depression. Anger. Anxiety. Sleep disturbance. Psychic or emotional numbing. Cynicism and distrust of government and authority. Concern with humanistic values overlaid with hedonism. Hypersensitivity to justice. A tendency to fits of rage. Fear of losing others. Fantasies of destruction.

"Sounds a lot like you the last time you quit smoking," his wife said, risking a little joke.

"But don't you see the ramifications of that list?"

"The ramifications? I don't know. Do you think you're experiencing Post-Traumatic Stress Disorder?"

"That's the crazy thing. Who knows? At my age, how can you tell? At my age, how's a guy supposed to know whether he's finally suffering from Post-Traumatic Stress or having a midlife crisis or just drinking too much coffee?"

"Well, don't let a little midlife crisis spoil your whole evening. How about a glass of wine?"

"Eat, drink and be a happy basket case."

"How many of those symptoms apply to you, anyway?"

"I don't know. Either none of them or a lot of them. I mean, I wonder how intense those feelings have to be before they count? That is, when I think about punk rock, video music and the size of our house payment, I get pretty depressed. When I think about the Middle East, Central America and the candidates running for president, I feel anxiety clear down to my toes. And of course when I think about the tragic deterioration of the Cleveland Indians, I get

164

so angry I could become a Cubs fan. Fortunately, I still have too much self-respect to do that."

"A little depression, anger and anxiety are probably good for you."

"But how am I supposed to know if my anger, anxiety, depression and all that other stuff is genuine, or if it's just coffee nerves, or if they're actually deep hang-ups about midlife or Vietnam? Maybe I should cut down to two cups of coffee a day and see what happens."

"I suppose you could talk to a shrink, if being calm and sane means that much to you."

"Nah. Having one more bill to pay would just make me that much more depressed, angry and anxious. You know how I get about money."

"You know, the more I look at this list, the more I don't think you have to worry about being in the throes of a midlife crisis or Delayed Stress."

"How's that?"

"Listen: Depression. Anger. Anxiety. Sleep disturbance. Emotional numbing. Hypersensitivity. Cynicism and distrust of government. Difficulty with authority figures. Fear of losing others. A tendency to fits of rage. Fantasies of destruction. Do you know, I have all those feelings myself every now and then."

"Maybe it's contagious."

"No. Considering what's going on in the world, it's not contagious, simply appropriate."

165

I Love . . .
I Hate . . .

September 24, 1982

I love . . .

Potatoes. The Cleveland Indians. The Miami Dolphins. PBS' "Butterflies." Listening to music in the dark. The time of month my favorite magazines come out. The atmosphere at airports. The thrill of catching two green lights in a row. Actors without a cause.

I hate . . .

People who oversimplify the complex. People who complicate the simple. People who give compliments that depress you. People whose jobs require them to deal constantly with the public but who act like they don't like people. Actors with a cause.

I love . . .

Drivers who let me pull out into traffic ahead of them.

I hate . . .

Drivers ahead of me who hold me up by letting other cars pull out into traffic ahead of them.

I love . . .

Former guv Bob Bennett's goatee. Wichita Aero player Shooty Babbit's name. Autumn "football weather." Streets without potholes. Streets without detours. Businesses without portable signs.

I hate . . .

Nasty winters. Conversations, TV shows, books and just about anything else having to do with dieting. People who have snobbish attitudes about eating and drinking. People so obsessed with their health and/or bodies that they all but

166

start a religious sect devoted to it/them. Intersections without stop or yield signs.

I love . . .

Saturday nights. Discovering great new playgrounds while driving around with our kids. Books so good you wish they'd never end.

I hate . . .

Almost everything at a salad bar except the salad and dressing. The taste of milk. Tea. Surly people. Anonymous nasty letters. Light bulbs when they burn out (Why do they always burn out when you try to switch them on instead of after they've been on a while?).

I love . . .

Seeing couples over the ripe old age of 25 who look like they're still in love (with each other). Going for long walks where there are no people. Going for walks where there are huge crowds of people. The smell of burning fireplaces, the smell of barbecues, and most of all, the smell of burning leaves in autumn.

I hate . . .

Couples who put each other down in front of other people. Having to get knots out of our kids' shoelaces. Gossip (well-l-l-l, ill-spirited gossip, anyway). Waiting for trains. Waiting in lines. Waiting for doctors. Waiting.

I love . . .

The sound of a bat hitting a baseball. The sound of a basketball swishing cleanly through a net. The feel of a good overhead smash in tennis. Watching a long touchdown run. Watching a triple. And, as much as I hate to admit it, a knockout in boxing.

I hate . . .

Soccer. Scuffing the toes of new shoes for the first time. Ballpoint pens whose points wiggle when you write. Hospital lobbies. Any kind of waiting room.

I love . . .

The beer commercials featuring ex-jock types.

I hate . . .

The commercials that suggest that the key to friendship, friendly competition, love and maybe even life itself is choosing the right beer "to live by."

I love . . .

Traveling by car. Traveling by plane. Traveling.

I hate . . .

World-weary 16-year-olds. People who seem to get their jollies being either sincere, solemn or irate. Columns that end with a whimper rather than a "Bang!"

———

Good Neighbor Jack

August 5, 1985

I never saw the movie "Good Neighbor Sam," but however sensational a neighbor this guy Sam was, I'd give you odds not to mention ends that our neighbors Jack and Evadna are far better.

And it's not what you think.

After we moved into our house about five years ago, they never spoiled us or anything like that by begging us constantly to let them sit with our kids or insisting we let them cook all our meals for us.

No. They're good neighbors because they're good people. Warm. Upbeat. Thoughtful. Not that Evadna doesn't make good cookies, too.

With people like Jack and Evadna in a neighborhood, property values ought to be higher. So when you sell, you can advertise, "FOR SALE – Home sweet home. 3 BR, grge, and 4-star neighbors worth $10,000."

Jack and Evadna are perfect neighbors. And they not only loved our kids, which is always nice, but they even seemed to like me.

They never borrowed anything from us. But we sure borrowed things from them.

And Jack was always strolling over when he saw me laboring away outside to tell me to be careful, compliment me for continuing my struggle to act domesticated and offer tactful homeowner-type tips.

Then it wasn't much more than a year ago when my car, the world's ugliest and meanest machine, wouldn't start. While I stood there trying to glare it started, Jack came strolling slowly over.

"Won't start, eh?" he said.

Next thing I knew, he had made three or four slow trips back and forth to his house, was down under the hood performing surgery, and, finally, he got the car humming so agreeably I half expected it to apologize.

Jack is 83. I suppose Evadna must be about that age, too, but the years have been remarkably kind to her.

They bought a camper just a few years ago when Jack was almost 80. That gives you an idea of their spirit and energy.

About three years ago, they painted their house themselves. Scraped it, too. Went at it early every morning, stopped when the sun got hot.

Jack was with the Wichita Art Association for 43 years, 23 years as head of the ceramics department. An outstanding ceramist, lithographer and painter, he received the art association's Medal of Honor.

But when I think of Jack, I picture him riding up the street on his old bike early in the morning, getting his exercise, and sometimes stopping to ask me how my car was running or maybe grumble congenially about politics.

But last winter was brutal for Jack. He had a series of mild strokes.

Our street hasn't been the same this summer without him. No more bike riding. No more driving. He has to use a walker. But the spirit was still there. It really irked him that he wasn't allowed to drive.

All this summer he got worse. Evadna's health suffered from taking care of him. It couldn't go on like that much longer.

Things happened fast last week. Our telephone rang Friday morning as I was getting ready to go to work. We went next door right away.

Jack and Evadna were leaving in a couple of hours for Manhattan, Kan. Evadna would move in with her daughter. Jack would go into a nursing home there. He did not like the idea. But he understood.

In their living room, Evadna sat on the sofa, looking exhausted. Jack sat in a chair, gazing straight ahead, his walker in front of him.

Everybody was fighting back tears.

"I hope you never have to go through anything like this," Evadna said.

Jack's eyes were wide, and he blinked and blinked.

"We've been together 64 years," Evadna said, stopping, swallowing, wiping her eyes. "I'm telling you this isn't easy."

We talked a while more. But I had to go to work. Jack lifted his unsteady, pale left hand, and we shook hands a second time.

"I wish I could die," he said. "I hate being like this."

"Give it a fight, Jack. Get better so you can come home."

We went to the door. My wife said, "I have to drop Bob

off at work. His car won't start."

Evadna smiled. She said, "Too bad Jack can't fix it for you."

Sure is. But he can give me a hand next time, after he's better and comes back.

And until then, the old neighborhood won't be nearly as nice.

(NOTE: John "Jack" Leland Pharo, 88, passed away July 8, 1991, in Manhattan, Kan.)

———

Mom

February 8, 1989

Except for her distinctive brown hair and familiar, snazzy glasses, the woman lying in the coffin, surrounded by flowers, her hands resting on an open, tattered old Bible, did not look much like my mother at all.

Lying there in the Frain Mortuary on South Riverside Drive in Winamac, Ind., just up the hill from the tree-lined Tippecanoe River, my mother did not remotely resemble the worn-out, wasted woman I'd just spent nine days with in Pulaski County Memorial Hospital.

Astonishingly, she looked 20 to 25 years younger than she had the evening she died, Jan. 23, 1989, at 66. She looked, in fact, beautiful.

Mom, a proud woman even on her worst and weakest days, would have been very pleased at how good Dan Frain had made her look.

Amyloidosis, a rare, terminal, degenerative disease, had left her once-hefty body withered away to 70-some pounds, and her face in the end was gray, wrinkled and twisted with pain. Yet, amazingly, she now looked like an attractive,

171

smooth-skinned, middle-aged woman.

You have to know a little about what my mother went through the last several years to understand how amazing this seemed.

Eleven years before, when the amyloidosis was first diagnosed, Mom was given six months to two years to live.

If it was a testimony to her character that she lived so much longer, the price she paid was almost faith-shakingly high.

The pain she suffered, despite her high-powered medication, was so excruciating all those years that she often would lie in bed doubled up, moaning, clenching her teeth and clutching pillows tightly to her stomach.

Dozens of times, she was rushed to hospital emergency rooms, seemingly on the brink of death, only to bounce back.

With the pain, she suffered dizzy spells and sometimes fell. And the last years, her internal bleeding became so severe she needed regular blood transfusions to keep going.

At the age of 55, a sturdy, hardy woman turned into a frail old lady who, finally, this year, longed to die to escape the pain.

But Mom was some woman to behold. She lived with my family in Wichita a few years after the illness was first diagnosed, then moved back to Winamac into a rest home, where, despite her pain, she proudly proceeded to take care of herself, put 100,000 miles on an exercise bike, read omnivorously, study and get involved in a network of amyloidosis patients who wrote each other.

The closest she ever seemed to come to self-pity was when she wondered what awful thing she might have done in her life to deserve to suffer such intense, unrelenting pain.

But Mom's life was a good one, probably even by saints' standards.

172

After divorcing my dad, she devoted herself to her three kids and her own parents. Because her fellow church members had told her that her divorce would be acceptable in God's eyes only if she never married again, she never considered it.

Without a high school diploma or work experience, she went to a beauticians' school, opened a beauty shop in our small home, worked in it five days a week, spent Sundays and Mondays helping out her parents on their farm outside town, and she kept up this pace for years.

Getting no child support or alimony, some weeks she cleared as little as $45 in her shop. But we always ate, always got new clothes each school year, and never did it enter my mind once during those years that, moneywise, we might have been considered poor.

Mom was the epitome of efficiency, the opposite of me.

I'm sure she never paid a bill a minute late in her life. She never forgot a birthday, anniversary, holiday or oil change. She saved everything. She not only saved some junk mail, she filed it. She collected all those strange Avon bottles, hoping they would "be worth a lot of money someday." And somehow she managed to put aside money each week to shop for Christmas, her favorite time of year.

During Mom's last days, the amyloidosis totally ravaged her, intensifying to the very end. But the disease didn't destroy her completely. Her dignity and her faith never failed her.

Can you tell I'm proud I'm Helen Getz's son?

Thoughts I Couldn't
Put a Stop to . . .

How come I don't really believe it when some people say they're bored by pornography and/or sleazy dancers?

•

Even if my watches are "waterproof" or "water resistant," I've never worn them swimming or in the shower.

•

Probably the worst movie ever made: "Great Balls of Fire."

•

Probably the worst acting ever done: Dennis Quaid as Jerry Lee Lewis in "Great Balls of Fire."

•

If I could be any age forever, I'd pick anywhere from 34 to 36.

•

Many authors are very bad at reading their own stuff aloud.

•

Maybe the only actor I really miss – Peter Sellers.

•

If a model has to do a job over again, is that called remodeling?

•

How come you find so much exercise equipment – exercycles, weights and weight benches, mostly – at garage sales?

FUN (AHEM) & GAMES

"Compared with Bob Knight's coaching style and raging temper tantrums, the Seven Last Plagues will be fun."

1985

About Those W's, L's, O's, M's and Dingers . . .

June 9, 1989

Thanks for that charming weather report, Garth. And now, here he is with Channel 1's Sunday spectacular sports action report . . . Bob!

Well, thanks, Boopsi!

Well . . . Bob! I guess there sure were a lot of games and stuff played again today in sports, right?

Right you are, Boopsi! And if I hurry, maybe I can squeeze the scores of a few of those games in before I get to my special weekly video feature I love so much, Sports Bloopers and Blunders wherein some of the world's greatest athletes are shown week after week after week falling down and getting hit on the head and stuff like that when what you really want to know is more details about the Lakers' game!

Go for it, Bob!

Well, today in the Bigs, Boopsi, lots of W's and L's!

In the senior circuit, the 'stros bombed the 'pos, the Pods nipped the Cubbies, the Bucs edged the R's, and over in the junior loop, the M's got a big W against the O's, the A's blasted the Brew Crew and the Twinkies pounded the Pale Hose!

Now going to K.C., the Royals were swinging big sticks today, led by Bo Jackson, who smashed two dingers and had five ribbies!

Then, in hoops, the NBA playoffs are . . .

Bob?

What? What, Boopsi? You're not supposed to interrupt my sportscast! What is it? A major bulletin just in?

Bob, I'm just curious. Did you say the the M's picked up a big W against the L's, or the A's picked up a big M against the L's?

Well, the M's got a W against the O's, Boopsi!

And what does that sporty alphabet soup mean, Bob?

What? Well, uh, W's are wins and L's are losses. That's all.

But what about the M's and the A's and the O's and the Brew Crew, Bob? What are all those initials and funny names?

Well, Boopsi, the M's are the Mariners, the A's are . . .

AAAAAAAAAAAAHHHH! I can't take it anymore! What are we talking about here, Bob? What in the heck have you been jabbering about all these months! What's a dish? What are the "Bigs"? How come some of you sports guys talk like that so much! You say dinger! You're a dinger!

Boopsi, Boopsi! Sports fans understand! And by using a lot of slang and nicknames, by calling *everything* something *else*, I add a lot of *color* to my report, not to mention I also sound real sportily *hip!*

But that's DUMB, Bob. I've been meaning to tell you. That's REALLY dumb. Why don't you talk like the rest of us, Bob? Use WORDS! Real words and WHOLE words! Sports fans don't sit around saying "dingers!"

Boopsi! Calm down!

Why, Bob, why, why, why don't you EVER say "home run" instead of dinger?! You ALWAYS say DINGER! Bo hit another dinger! Strawberry hit a GRAND dinger! You NEVER say home run or homer!

But, Boopsi! I . . . I . . .

And BOARDS, Bob. Why always boards? Why don't you EVER say rebounds? And must you always say HOOPS instead of basketball?

Boopsi! Part of the beauty of sports is its wonderful vernacular!

Jargon is always nice, Bob. But if you get any worse with your slang, we're going to have to start running subtitles while you talk!

I'll bet some people are impressed, Boopsi! They probably say, "Look! Bob just went the whole month without saying 'home run' or 'Mariners' or 'rebound' even once! He's good!"

But, Bob, what if I recited the news the way you talk? Think about it: "Well, folks, around Wichita tonight in traffic accident action, there were three big A's, or accidents, with two tragic F's, or fatalities, and four gory I's – injuries. The worst big smasheroo was at the exciting intersection of Rock 'n' 'Logg, that's Rock Road and Kellogg, where there was this real metal-masher. Elsewhere on the P.E., or Planet Earth, scene, Iran's main man, the Crazy K, Khomeini, was deep-sixed today despite the all-out efforts of his devoted followers to tear him to shreds first!" So what do you say to this, Bob?

I don't know. AAAAAAHHHHHHH, maybe?

Well put. Gimme five, Bucko.

———

Moral: Never Punch a Marshmallow Salesman

June 11, 1980

Ever notice that when newspaper writers refer to the most recent adversary that temperamental baseball manager Billy Martin punched, they always refer to the punchee as a "marshmallow salesman"?

Being of sound mind and having better things to do, you

probably never gave it much thought. But I have.

Think about it. Here it is, nine months after the last Martin fist landed, and writers still refer to the punchee not only as a salesman but specifically as a salesman of marshmallows.

That should have taught Martin a lesson. And the rest of us, too.

Never punch a marshmallow salesman.

Why?

Because it sounds terrible. Worse, it sounds terrible and sort of funny at the same time.

If the punchee were, say, a power tools salesman, do you think newspaper writers would always faithfully call him a power tools salesman? No way. They'd simply call him a salesman and let it go at that, usually.

But a marshmallow salesman? That's a once-in-a-lifetime opportunity for writers. Marshmallow is one of those wonderful, loaded words that, all by themselves, lend a sense of fun or titillation to what otherwise might be a straight, dry story.

The very word, however subtly, brightens the dullest sentence – unless, of course, the sentence happens to be about a wiener roast or a shopping list.

All by itself it sort of sounds like a joke – Have you heard the one about the tipsy baseball manager and the marshmallow salesman?

Actually, that could have been a lead paragraph on a *straight* news story about what happened between Martin and the punchee. And the next paragraph, containing the specifics, would have been the, ah, punch line.

But there's more to "marshmallow salesman" than that – sorry. When you read that Martin, the world's oldest *enfant terrible*, hauled off and socked a marshmallow salesman, you could – if you really wanted to – picture this red-nosed barroom brawler (Martin) towering over this tiny marshmallow, which is carrying a salesman's sample case in one stick-like little arm and a sales pad in the other. Then Billy clobbers the little thing, sending it flying.

It just sounds terrible, that's all, hitting a marshmallow salesman – even though we can't quite help grinning. Somehow, hitting a marshmallow salesman sounds almost as bad as hitting a woman or a child – or a powder puff salesman!

Now if Battlin' Billy had hit a vacuum cleaner salesman or a magazine salesman or an encyclopedia salesman, some of us might have applauded and even yelled, "Hit 'im harder next time, Martin!" But Billy didn't do that. He had to go and hit the guy who might be the only living marshmallow salesman on the face of the earth.

It's just too bad Billy didn't hit a heavy-equipment salesman, which sounds so much more impressive. Even though a heavy-equipment salesman might have been much smaller than the marshmallow salesman, a heavy-equipment salesman sort of sounds like a guy who's a sumo wrestler-looking, 6-foot-3, 250-pound redneck who probably started the fight in the first place, right? But Billy had to hit a marshmallow salesman.

I guess that's life, though.

We have no control over who sits down on the bar stool next to us.

Maybe Woody Hayes
Wasn't Ideal Role Model

January 10, 1979

I took the news of Woody Hayes' firing pretty hard.

How could Ohio State University do that to poor Woody? Fire him as a football coach after all these years?

All he did was sock some unsuspecting Clemson University player in the throat during the Gator Bowl game.

I ask you. Is that so terrible? And the player was only a linebacker.

Another thing. What's so special about Clemson's players, anyway? Are they above being assaulted, for crying out loud?

Woody Hayes made a career out of physically abusing people, and nobody ever fired him before. That's just the way Woody is. High-strung.

Let's see. In his time, Woody ripped down sideline downs markers, kicked yardage markers, threw his coat into the stands, crushed his eyeglasses in his hand, stomped on his wristwatch, tore up some of his hats, socked a fan, threw a projector at his assistants, slapped one reporter, shoved another, punched a TV cameraman in the tummy, swung at a reporter and missed, and who knows what else.

How can you help but admire a man like that?

You can see why I was so distraught that I reacted the way I did when I first heard the news of his firing on TV.

I slammed a lamp to the floor and stomped on it.

I kicked a yardage marker – disciples of the Woody Hayes Philosophy of Life always keep a 50-yard line marker handy for moments of stress.

181

I socked somebody – I was so mad I didn't notice who – but I haven't seen my wife around for quite some time, now.

Then I stormed into my bedroom, slammed the door the way Woody used to slam his locker room door after defeats, and refused to talk to anybody.

My idol, fired? With Woody gone from the 50-yard line to the unemployment line, whom am I to idolize? Sinatra has mellowed. Billy Martin is in exile. Idi Amin, maybe?

Hardly had I begun to cool off when this newspaper, the very newspaper I work for, came out with a scathing editorial, actually finding fault with Woody's behavior.

Well, needless to say, I was beside myself when I went to work the next day.

I would have slammed my wristwatch to the floor and stomped on it like Woody, but I didn't because I can't afford a new one. So, instead, I threw desk-neighbor Judy Stanley's watch to the floor and stomped on *it,* nearly breaking her wrist. Crawling to the phone, Judy phoned the security guards.

Next, I kicked the yardage marker I keep by my desk.

Then I socked Frank Good, who was handy. He socked me back and phoned security.

After I got off the floor, I roared, "Why didn't this newspaper defend Woody's behavior? Why? Why? Why?"

Moving right down the row, I socked Jon Roe in the throat, waking him up.

Jon socked me back and phoned security.

After I got off the floor, I ranted, "Everything that I am, I owe to Woody Hayes! I patterned myself after this extremely successful man!

"His philosophy is my philosophy – 'If at first you don't succeed, throw something. If further frustrated, kick your yardage marker! And if, finally, you still don't succeed, *hit* somebody!' "

Then the security guards came and took me away.

Now I admire Woody Hayes more than ever. He held a job 28 years doing stuff the rest of us couldn't get away with for five minutes.

Ah, sports.

————

The Raging Creature of Indiana Basketball

January 20, 1988

If you enjoy a good horror story, and you're not the least bit squeamish, have I got a book for you.

I've just finished reading this extraordinary story, a great, almost stunning book I predict is destined to become a classic, a work of fiction so sublimely terrifying it will make your spine tingle like a xylophone and cause your palms to sweat so bad you'll think you've come down with a case of monsoons.

The name of the book bound to be a classic in the same league with "Frankenstein," "Dr. Jekyll and Mr. Hyde" and "One Flew Over the Cuckoo's Nest" is "A Season on the Brink," by John Feinstein.

Feinstein's wonderfully imaginative and memorable main character is a college basketball coaching tyrant named Bob Knight.

Compared with Knight's coaching style and raging temper tantrums, the Seven Last Plagues will be fun.

Feinstein's Knight berates, abuses and lambastes everybody. He rants; he raves; he insults his players repeatedly and despicably; he jerks everybody around by playing ludicrous, almost childish mind games; he throws fits, tantrums

183

and chairs, kicks megaphones, sulks, appears insistent upon dominating and bullying all who would dare venture close to his little hoop-and-hardwood world; and even more alarmingly, he can act this way without losing his self-control.

It should be noted, though, that the man has an endearing side, great generosity of spirit and an intense sense of loyalty to friends – provided, apparently, they don't look at him wrong or something.

What's especially impressive about Feinstein's work of fiction is how convincingly he presents it as a non-fiction account of Indiana University's 1985-86 basketball season.

But, of course, no way could this book be true. Right? I mean, what self-respecting, civilized major university would let a coach behave like that?

So Feinstein apparently has turned out a sports version of what Gore Vidal calls a historical novel, mixing fact and fiction for the sake of a more powerful story.

And because this compelling horror story is such an impressive work of imagination, I thought it might be amusing to make up some appropriate "book jacket blurbs" from famous people, dead or alive, that could go on the cover of future editions:

Genghis Khan – "A wonderful book! Inspiring! What a refreshing character, this Bob Knight! He coaches teams like I treated villages that got in my way."

Dr. Benjamin Spock, famous kiddie specialist – "I've dealt with a lot of people who behave like that. Usually, though, they're 4 years old."

Idi Amin – "And people thought *I* was scary."

Miss Manners – "Is it, I mean he, even housebroken?"

John Wooden, former great UCLA basketball coach and gentleman from Indiana – "I guess Bob Knight gives new meaning to the old Indiana basketball term 'Hoosier Hysteria.' In fact, he gives new meaning to the word hysteria."

Supreme Court Justice Byron White – "If all coaches acted like that, we'd have to consider making it illegal to coach basketball."

Bob Barker, famous game show host and animal lover – "I had a pit bull like that once."

The famous wild man of Borneo – "One would think Mr. Knight does not possess the emotional wherewithal to win without intimidating."

The Marquis de Sade – "Sometimes this coaching fellow just isn't nice."

Attila the Hun – "When it comes to leadership and style, he has the right idea. But if I had to give Bob Knight any advice, it would be, 'Lighten up.' "

Dr. James Naismith – "It's all my fault! I take all the blame. If I'd known somebody like this was going to come along and turn my nice, fun game into a device for torturing youth, I'd never have invented basketball!"

Once Upon a Time in Kansas

April 6, 1988

This is the stuff of storybooks.

Aesop's Fables. The Brothers Grimm. Arabian Nights. Lewis Carroll.

This is the stuff, the certifiable stuff, of magic, myths and miracles.

It can't be true.

Don't try to tell me the 27-11ish Kansas Jayhawks actually beat the big, bad, runnin', gunnin', rootin', tootin'

185

Oklahoma slam-bam-wham-jam, in-your-face, up-your-nose, eat-my-dust, show-no-mercy, take-no-prisoners Sooners.

No way, ho-ho-Jose. It is to laugh.

Teams that have lost 11 games don't receive NCAA championship trophies and rings, they receive condolences and get-well cards.

Kansas 83, Oklahoma 79?

Sure. And cows fly.

If KU really beat OU, isn't almost anything possible, might there not be unicorns and mermaids and leprechauns?

Readers who aren't basketball fans might not understand the magnitude of this supposed victory.

The Sooners are, as they say, baaad. Which is to say, great.

They didn't just schedule games this year, they declared them.

The Sooners didn't just play to win, they didn't just play to score 100 points, they played to win and score 100 points and smash their opponents into little whimpering smudges on the floor.

To the Sooners and their Dr. Frankensteinian coach, Billy Tubbs, annihilation and total humiliation only make victory that much sweeter. Their game plan is to tear the wings off opponents first, then squash them as hard as they can.

The Sooners, 35-4 if that game really happened, averaged about 103 points a game and beat opponents by an average of 23 points a game this season. Count Dracula didn't have that kind of killer instinct. OU was college basketball's version of "Jaws." With OU anywhere around, it wasn't safe to go into a ball game.

Their swarming, suffocating, wall-to-wall defense was the next best thing to throwing a net over a team. Trying to play Oklahoma on offense was like trying to play basketball dressed in straitjackets.

And their relentless, non-stop offense always reminded me of Pearl Harbor. Ka-boom, ka-boom! Smart opponents didn't guard OU, they ran for cover and hoped an NBA team would come rushing to the rescue.

Monday night's game figured to be the next best thing to a disaster movie, to rank in history not with other NCAA finals but instead with events like the San Francisco earthquake and the great Chicago fire – with KU as the pathetic victims.

That is, as great horrors go, you've got famines, pestilence, earthquakes, floods and the Sooners.

Could it actually be that KU won?

Can you tame a tornado, halt a hurricane, shut off a flash flood?

It seems KU did.

So we are talking storybook stuff, minor miracles.

Danny Manning, the young man with the rhyming name, was also poetry in motion.

With a little help and a lot of hustle from his teammates and some superb coaching, Manning exterminated Oklahoma.

Thirteen field goals, five free throws, 18 bountiful rebounds, 31 wonderful points.

Never have I seen a player who looked more determined to win or more confident than Manning on Monday night.

The way he moved, the way he sometimes brought the ball across midcourt. The almost unnervingly nonchalant way he flicked oncoming passes from teammates right back at them, playground style, without catching them. The way he loped into position. The way he seemed to see the championship as his personal Manifest Destiny.

The 6-foot-10 senior did what only a rare few of the

greatest college stars have managed to do in NCAA tournaments with games on the line – take charge, assert himself, carry his team all the way. . . .

Once upon a time in Kansas.

———

Was Wilt Just Afraid of the Dark?

December 15, 1991

"Bob Getz:

"We would like very much to have you write an article on Wilt Chamberlain's conquest of 20,000 females. . . . Thank you."

You want me to write a column about somebody's love life?

What kind of columnist do you take me for?

I run a respectable, tasteful article here. No matter what anybody says.

I'm not into cheap, tacky, tawdry, sleazy, sensationalistic trash, just because that sort of thing appeals to so many readers' prurient interests and increases readership tenfold. . . .

Hmmm. Tenfold? Oh, all right. If you insist.

I suppose I do have an obligation to deal with such items, especially because I have a background in sportswriting.

But I warn you. You'll just have to control your disappointment when I'm really tasteful about this.

Actually, I haven't read Wilt's book and don't plan to. I thought I'd just wait for the Jay Leno jokes.

Who needs to read it, anyway? Wilt's out on the talk show trail, so everybody is commenting on the book's good parts – I mean, the disgustingly tacky, chest-thumping, locker-room Lothario parts.

And all I can say is, based on what I've read, I'm impressed.

I never would have guessed Wilt was such a friendly guy.

From what I'd read about his tropical-storm-like surliness back when he was playing pro basketball, I didn't think anybody liked him, except maybe some of his parents. I got the impression his teammates didn't even like being at the same end of the basketball court with him.

Obviously, I was wrong.

The guy had to be pretty doggoned friendly to hit it off with 20,000 ladies and then know them in the biblical sense.

Those among us who haven't known 20,000 women in the biblical sense know it's actually not all that easy just getting to know 20,000 people in any sense at all, biblically or un-biblically.

Heck. I doubt I've even passed 20,000 strangers on the streets in my lifetime. Or nodded at more than 15 or 16.

So obviously Wilt was an almost unstoppably friendly guy.

Either that or unstoppably lonely.

Unless he was just afraid of the dark.

Maybe he picked up a woman every night because it was a lot less embarrassing than having to buy a night-light.

Wilt's amorous statistics, reportedly, average out to 1.2 shall-we-say new friends each day over 40 years.

Do you realize the logistics involved there?

Some of his apparently interchangeable pals must have been running into each other coming and going.

Maybe he had a revolving door. A shuttle bus to his home. A waiting room.

The towels in his bathroom must have been marked HIS

and THEIRS.

But the most baffling thing to me is how he maintained his off-court scoring average of 1.2 dalliances a day without getting involved in some average-killing, may-I-see-you-again? relationships.

Maybe Wilt's idea of real intimacy isn't actual hanky-panky itself but something deeper, more satisfying, like giving a special lady his autograph on her way out and saying, "Hey, I'd really love to see you again tomorrow, baby, but I don't want to hurt my average."

Or maybe he's just looking for love and is a lot more selective (if at first you don't succeed, tryst, tryst again) than most.

Amazing – 1.2 liaisons per day. No wonder Wilt was one of the worst free-throw shooters in NBA history. Free throws require concentration, and how could the poor guy ever concentrate?

He had to be terribly preoccupied, thinking about how he was going to score after each game ended, while always trying not to lose count of his conquest total.

Imagine if poor, egomaniacal Wilt, aiming for 20,000, had ever lost count and had to start over.

Thoughts I Couldn't Put a Stop to . . .

Who gave the first high five?

•

I keep waiting for some young, irreverent rock singer to write a song called "Where Have You Gone, Mr. Coffee?"

•

How come the best, most successful basketball coaches so often seem so joyless?

•

How come no bowler has come along and captured the masses' fancy, boosting pro bowling's popularity something like Arnold Palmer did for golf?

•

Just joking: Have you heard that Oral Roberts University's basketball team has an 8-foot center?
The only trouble is, Oral Roberts is the only person who can see him.

•

Did Pete Rose ever officially retire as a player?

•

I've never heard of a boxer who had a losing record.

•

What may be the hardest accomplishment in all of pro sports? Pronouncing Martina Navratilova.

THE SMOKING SECTION

"Cats are even dumber than cows. When was the last time you had to call the fire department because your cow climbed a telephone pole and couldn't get down?"

1992

What Kind of Fool Are Smokers?

November 18, 1987

Smoky, hazy reflections of a once-devout, now-reformed smoker on the day before the Great American Smokeout . . .

Ever wonder why Frank Sinatra, Dean Martin and Sammy Davis all don't have lung cancer or emphysema?

Every time you used to see them singing on television, they were always puffing away on cigarettes like nicotine fiends. . . .

Strangers in the niiiiight (short, quick drag) . . . *exchanging glances, lovers at first siiiight* (exhale – with great feeling) . . .

Or:

Ev'er-bud-dy loves some-bud-dy sommme-time (quick puff, squint with devastating suavity, exhale) . . . *Makes no dif-rinse* . . .

Or:

What kind of fool am I (inhale coolly, tilt head to a very hip angle, exhale, snap fingers a couple of times) . . . *who never fell in lovvvve* (gesture despairingly with cigarette, its wispy smoke creating major romantic ATMOSPHERE) . . .

Remember those days? Frank, Dino and Sammy all used cigarettes like props, virtually setting their own trademark-like moods by smoking while they sang.

Watching them warble, croon and bellow was like watching a four-alarm fire, set to music.

But I found it reassuring, seeing them smoke up a storm. The way I saw it, if they were such heavy, almost non-

194

stop smokers that they couldn't stand to go more than two or three phrases in a song without taking a toe-deep, lung-filling, mind-spinning drag, and they were all getting up there in years, then didn't it only follow that I, too, could keep smoking and reach their age someday without getting lung cancer or emphysema?

I mean, if they could inhale all that glorious poison over the years and still not be in oxygen tents at their ages, then maybe I had a chance to live to be at least 35 or 40.

Except I was no good at kidding myself – at least about that.

So I decided that if I really wanted to take my best shot at living to be 1,000, or at least 35, I had two alternatives:

Either quit smoking altogether, cold turkey.

Or not quit completely, but smoke only while singing "Strangers in the Night" in front of audiences.

I took the easier way out. Rather than quit completely, I decided to smoke only when begged to sing "Strangers" in front of audiences.

I recommend this way of cutting down on your smoking. It's been eight years now since I last puffed a cigarette.

I call it the Dooby-Dooby-Don't-Smoke Method.

By the way, have you heard the latest in the ongoing battle between smokers and anti-smokers for public turf?

Airlines are talking about banning smoking completely on flights.

Now I know that's a good, healthy idea. But considering the way planes have been crashing and having near-collisions in the overcrowded, over-friendly skies, it strikes me as darkly ironic that airlines may be more worried about the air inside their planes than the air outside the planes.

Wouldn't it be interesting if smokers, seeking consistency, started a crusade to get a flying ban until the wildly deregulated skies are much safer?

195

deregulated skies are much safer?

Imagine an anti-flying activist picketing an airport and getting into a conversation with a non-smoking flier:

"Excuse me, sir. You still fly? After the air tragedies we've had and all the near-misses? Are you crazy? How heavy a flier are you, sir?"

"Oh, I take five, six flights a month."

"What? That's awful! Do you realize the risks you're taking? Do you know even the surgeon general gets white knuckles when he flies? While we non-fliers don't have to worry at all about being in a plane crash? Sir, I suggest you quit flying until the skies are safe."

"Well, I'm trying to cut down. But I can't quit completely."

"Well, it's your life. But you should think of your family."

"Hey! You should talk! You smoke!"

"I don't inhale anymore, though."

"Well, we're even, then. When I fly, I don't inhale, either. Or exhale. I hold my breath 'til I get where I'm going."

Interesting times we live in, aren't they?

Airlines are making the air safer to breathe.

But not safer to fly in.

(Sammy Davis died May 16, 1990, at age 64, of throat cancer.)

Quitting Smoking Is Like Being Dead, Only Worse

April 24, 1979

Colleagues babble all around me.

Strangers keep ringing my phone at me. In fact, I think that's the phone ringing again right now. . . .

"Hello? Hello? Getz here. Anybody there? Hello."

Nobody there. It was just my ears again. Ringing.

Ringing, ringing, ringing.

I have picked up the telephone and answered my ears 15 times in the last two days.

Not only are my ears ringing, but they also amplify everything I hear and make my own voice sound as if I were born with an echo in my head.

It's terrible. My head feels like a seashell sounds. In fact, I wouldn't be surprised if you could hear the ocean by listening to my ears.

Everything around me is either ringing or ticking or tocking or clickety-clacking or babbling.

How long will this go on? I don't know.

The last time I quit smoking, the withdrawal torture went on for 10 days. That was my roughest withdrawal ever, but I was very proud of myself. No matter how loud anybody blinked his eyes or did other annoying, noisy stuff like turning pages, I never harmed anybody seriously.

After you quit smoking heavily, you become irritable. I went from four packs a day to no cigarettes. I am irritable. I try to keep to myself. Maybe I am dangerous. Walk by my desk and I will chase you, snarling and nipping at your heels.

Ah, geez. This is like being dead, only worse.

It's like being dead, but you don't have the advantages.

Have you ever read the accounts of people who supposedly died on an operating table and then returned to life?

Invariably, these ex-dead people say that when they "died," they felt a sense of peace and tranquillity come over them and also felt their spirit or something kinda drift out of their body and up to the ceiling where they hovered and *watched* their former body and everybody else down below.

Well. That's kinda how it is after a heavy smoker quits, cold turkey. Except for the part about peace and tranquillity.

I feel sorta detached, removed, and far, far away. It's probably a lot like feeling as if you're floating around up by the ceiling, trying to function in a haze or in a kind of sea of ringing, ticking, babbling and clicking.

But the worst part of the ringing in my ears is when the ringing is actually the telephone.

The voices on the phone pound at my half-numb mind, reverberating, echoing, distorting, and I have to concentrate fiercely to figure out what's being said.

The sounds come at me something like this: "Hellololololo, Bob-obobobob? Thisisisisis isisis . . . "

Now everybody who has phoned me this week will know why our conversations were so brief.

One thing, readerpersons, I am not exaggerating here. If you think I am, check with an ex-heavy smoker.

But you know the worst thing about all this? It's knowing that if I resume smoking, I'll have to go through this *again*.

That's almost enough to make me want to quit for good.

Fat City, No;
Fat Country, Yes

January 30, 1977

All women want to weigh 118 pounds.

Life has taught me that.

Women all want to weigh 118 pounds (or less) because that's what they all weighed when they graduated from high school.

But, alas, all women don't weigh 118. They weigh 135 instead.

Ordinarily, I am not given to making such generalizations, however neat and tidy generalizations always are. But I've gotten the distinct impression over the years that your average woman weighs 135 pounds and wants to weigh 118 (or less).

So what do women do when they have 17 (or more) unwanted pounds?

They talk about diets.

In the afternoons over cake and coffee, they talk about diets.

On breaks at work, they nibble on doughnuts and talk about diets.

Where there's discussion, presumably, there's hope.

But unbristle, nice ladies. I'm not picking on women only.

I'm picking on everybody.

Nobody weighs what he or she wants to. And, like women, all men are either overweight or underweight.

Men never talk about diets, though. To one another, anyway. Thank God. Talk about diets is boring.

What men do is play golf. Golf isn't quite as boring as talk about diets, and it might even help you lose weight. The man who, say, puts on 15 pounds during the winter can go out, and if he's determined enough to make the effort, play golf all spring, summer and fall and lose up to 3 pounds.

Then some people jog either to lose weight or fix up the way their weight looks. The only thing more boring than talking about diets is jogging.

Obviously, life really is rough. That's because nobody ever weighs what those weight charts in the doctor's office say we ought to.

Take women, again. They have to console themselves by telling one another, "What, are you kidding? No, I'm not really all that much overweight, Bertha. It's my height that's the problem. I'm too short for my weight. According to my doctor's chart, I ought to be taller than 5-6. I ought to be 6-foot-11. So I imagine, Bertha, that being too short is probably a glandular problem."

Not even the svelte models weigh what they should. They don't weigh 118. They always weigh 65 pounds. They are all 5-foot-9 and weigh 65 (with eyelashes).

While the women who weigh 135 envy the models who weigh 65, those poor models are only about one chef's salad away at all times from dying of starvation.

If people in India look like they're starving, we rush them out a nice CARE package.

If people in America look like they're starving, we take their pictures and pay them $500 an hour provided they don't spend any of that money on food.

Take Twiggy. Do you think she started out looking like that on purpose? No way. If she'd been ugly, they would have made her a United Fund-type poster girl: "See This Poor Girl! There Are Thousands More Like Her in the World! Be Generous! Send Money for Her and the Others."

But she was pretty, and the rest, as they say, is history.

Florida and Southern California may be the only places in the country where people seem prone to weigh what they prefer to weigh.

That's because Floridians and Southern Californians spend all their time in bathing suits at the beach. They keep their weight down so they won't be mistaken for whales and get harpooned by Captain Ahab.

The Midwest probably has a lot more overweight people per square inch than either Florida or Southern California. It's all because we Midwesterners don't have to worry about being harpooned in the ocean.

Maybe every state ought to have an ocean for inspiration.

Or, maybe a great Floridian named J. Andrew Mead was right when he told me, "If God wanted people to live in the Midwest, he would have had the Pilgrims land there."

Shocking Stuff Women Should Know About Men!

April 25, 1982

Brace yourself. What you see below is an excerpt from Joy Smothers' enlightening, astonishing new book, "Lots of Really Shocking Stuff About Men's Quirks That Every Woman Who Can Scrape Together $10.95 (Plus Tax) Ought to Know for Her Own Good!" Other excerpts ran in this newspaper last week.

Men and women are different, studies indicate.

As a rule, men are taller, stronger, heavier, hairier,

meaner, dumber, touchier, more selfish, more demanding and much less sensitive than women.

In other words, men are invariably big, silly, snorting, pompous, presumptuous, posturing oafs.

Kept in their place, however, men can be tolerable, and a few studies even insist that some men can be almost endearing at times.

Many women write me wanting to know how to attract men. I always answer, "Don't bother. Get yourself a pet and a nice hobby instead." But if a woman persists, I try to help.

First, if all a woman wants are dates with your average frothy, insecure swine of a male, she should just peroxide her hair, get a sweater three sizes too small, put on a very drafty miniskirt and spiked heels, and she'll have so many men wanting a date she'll have to tell them to take a number and wait their turn.

Studies show, however, that while men prefer to date blondes, they marry brunettes. Maybe that's why they say blondes have more fun. Because they're not married and don't have real responsibilities.

But the best way for women, whatever their intent, to attract men is to radiate self-confidence. But how, you ask, can I, an ultra-plump, plain, clumsy, dumb, shy, unmarried woman of 73, radiate self-confidence?

Easy. Become an expert in some field – car repairs, belly dancing, bird-watching, spiders, weightlifting, knitting – you'll see. Being an expert bird-watcher will result in your radiating so much self-confidence that you'll have to hire a bodyguard and social secretary.

Now, some insights about men:

• Men who are attracted to women with hourglass figures are sexist swine. Men who are attracted to women with stunning faces are narrow-minded, sexist oafs. The best men are the ones who appreciate a woman for whatever reasons she wants to be appreciated – for her intelligence, sense of humor, personality, talent, unblemished complexion, whatever.

• Real men make tender but passionate and unselfish whoopee 38 to 43 times a night, more if the woman wishes. Men who cannot show that much "affection" are pansies. But few men know that a woman isn't truly fulfilled unless her man makes whoopee with her at least 30 times a night. Sadly, most men, being selfish and quickly satiated, demand two to three hours' sleep a night.

• Men do not experience real feelings, the way women do. Hormones are responsible for men's many flaws and weaknesses. That is, while women have none of these hormones, a man has 652 that cause impatience, 1,728 that cause selfishness, 2,457,193 that cause irritability, 43 billion that cause hatred of housework, one that causes respect of women as people and none that causes understanding of women's thoughts and feelings.

• Though physically stronger, actually men are fragile weaklings, worthless, inferior and justifiably insecure. Because men are so pathetic, women who wish to mollycoddle them should understand the five phases adult males go through:

Upward, Ho! – Ages 21-35 or so. This is when men are filled with tension and anxiety as they try to succeed.

The Threshold – 35-44. This is when men are filled with tension and anxiety as they approach middle age.

Transition Time – 40-55. This is when men are filled with tension and anxiety as they think about the failures that they are and realize that they'll never amount to anything.

Autumn Time – 50-66. This is when men are filled with tension and anxiety because old age is approaching.

Slow Down Time – Retirement age. This is when men are filled with tension and anxiety because of regrets, resentment, despair and the selfish fear of dying.

Now, the obvious moral of this book's story: To paraphrase George Bernard Shaw's 'enry 'iggins, "Why can't a man be more like a woman?"

———

"This Is the Merkle Car, Bambi Speaking"

June 12, 1987

So there I was, driving home from work on First Street, just bopping happily along, fantasizing as usual that I was Mario Andretti blazing into the final straightaway at the Indy 500, about to take yet another checkered flag, when something caught my eye in the car on my left.

Some guy, riding alone in a nice, conservative, executive-type car, seemed to be having a ball behind his steering wheel. He was smiling like a fiend, laughing and seemed almost oblivious to traffic around him.

What the guy was doing that was so much fun was talking on a car phone.

Now ordinarily, you don't think that much about somebody talking on a car phone. After all, it is the 20th century, so it's no big deal to have a car phone if you have the money and it doesn't embarrass you.

But this particular guy was having such a good time, I found myself feeling a little guilty, like I was invading his privacy by driving along beside him and noticing him.

I wondered whether I should honk and yell, "Hey! I'm sorry to be driving along beside you while you're on the phone. I hope I'm not disturbing you. But I can't help being here. It's the speed limit's fault. But if my radio's bothering you, I can turn it down!"

Actually, I don't know about you, but I wouldn't want a phone in my car. Most of the time, I don't even want a phone in our house. But we need a phone at home, of course, in case something important comes up, like somebody needing to play an emergency tennis match.

Phones could destroy us, you know. An increasing number of cars have phones. Planes have phones for passengers. We can carry phones when we mow the grass. Phones come in briefcases so they can be carried everywhere. To lunch. To the hairstylist. To take out the garbage.

This is not good. It's like technology is turning on us. Up to a point, it made our lives easier. Now it has started robbing us of our privacy. Beepers are bad enough. There is almost nowhere to hide anymore from the dreaded telephone.

But anyway, there I was, homeward bound, when I had to slow down momentarily, and the guy on my left moved ahead a car length.

And what happens? In the next car on my left, there was a woman driving, and, lo and behold, she also was talking on a phone and was every bit as joyful and animated as the guy ahead of her. They just had to be talking to each other.

Now isn't there something downright decadent about this? Something just too deadly modern? Might the world end not with a bang or a whimper but with a busy signal?

Until that moment, I had thought of car phones primarily as business instruments. But no longer.

Can you imagine what it will be like when car phones become commonplace, virtually standard equipment in cars?

Say you're single and driving along. You see somebody in another car who looks eye-poppingly personable. You honk. He or she sizes you up. You get distinctly winked at. You smile. And then your fellow friendly motorist either yells a phone number at you or flashes a phone number with his or her fingers, so you can call up, get acquainted and see whether you hit it off, without even having to send over a drink.

"This is the Merkle car, Bambi speaking," the woman might answer.

"Hi," the guy might say. "Hey, I love your vanity tag."

"Thanks. I like your hubcaps."

"Say? Is that a can of tennis balls I see in your back window?"

"Yes! Do you play, too?"

"Only in major tournaments if the Queen of England comes to watch."

"Really! Wow, do we have a lot in common!"

"You know, Bambi. It's really easy to talk to you. Why, I feel like I've known you since . . . since I got my driver's permit!"

"Maybe it's like my wise old grandma used to say. Honk if you love tennis and make at least $50,000 a year."

Imagine other car phone possibilities:

"I'm sorry, but the number you have dialed has gone into the shop for a tune-up. At the honk, please leave your name and number."

And . . .

"I'm sorry, but the number you have dialed has been repossessed."

Jeannette Ewertz Isn't Somebody Else – Honest!

October 14, 1987

They couldn't break Jeannette Ewertz.

What a woman.

Try as they might, they couldn't get her to crack, couldn't get her to have even a minor nervous breakdown.

And what remarkable thing did Jeannette Ewertz do?

She actually came out of a license bureau joking and laughing!

I'm sorry I don't have pictures. But some things you just have to take on faith.

Don't get me wrong. I'm not one of those people who are anti-license bureau clerks. I know some license bureau clerks, and they are regular people, just like us. They have a sense of humor. They have feelings, compassion. They laugh. They cry. They foam at the mouth.

If anything, I sympathize with them. What job could be more brutal than having to deal with long lines of impatient, frothing, demented creatures who have all waited until precisely 11:30 a.m. the last day of the month to get their licenses renewed during their lunch hour?

But that's not what Jeannette Ewertz was doing. Ewertz needed to replace the driver's license she had misplaced, and it wasn't the end of the month when she went in.

"The first time I went in," she said, dryly, "I got rejected.

"After I stood in line approximately 20 minutes with my birth certificate, my Boeing ID and my credit cards, this lady told me I had to have two specific kinds of ID – and I only had one of those.

"They ought to make small-time criminals go through what I went through," Ewertz said. "They'd never break another law again."

Ewertz named the 13 kinds of "acceptable" ID – among them:

"You can show your marriage license," she said. "Unfortunately, I had a party after my divorce and tore mine up. You can use a military 214 form – whatever that is. I think it's a kind of insecticide.

"You can have a certified copy of a court order for a change of name! You can show your picture from a school yearbook, if it isn't more than 5 years old. Unfortunately, I've been out more like 20 years.

"Then you can show your current driver's license, but I couldn't do that, of course, because that's what I was there to replace.

"All I had that was on their list was my birth certificate. I showed them my Boeing ID with my picture on it and said, 'Doesn't that look like *me*?' It didn't matter.

"I had my Citibank card and my registration, but this lady said that according to KSA-246 or something, dated July 1, 1984, those kinds of ID aren't acceptable.

"Anyway, I left and went digging for another kind of ID. When I got back, I had to wait an hour and a half!

"When I finally got up there, I thought about telling them, 'Look, I'm trying to pull a fast one! Actually, I'm from the planet Nebulus, my antennae are underneath my hair and I'm trying to fool you and get a driver's license so I can go get some beer.'

"I don't know what they were thinking when they made those restrictions. What I do know is the law obviously doesn't allow these clerks to use their own common sense."

Ewertz got her new license, exiting joking.

"I'm going to take very good care of this one," she said. "I have it on a chain with a hole through it and wear it around my neck next to my St. Christopher."

I phoned the license bureau. A man named Gary Carter read me the same 13 kinds of ID that Ewertz said are acceptable.

"No exceptions?" I asked.

"There's one," Carter said. "You only need one ID if you can cite something we can check from your driving record, like how many speeding tickets you've had – information like that."

I wasn't able to contact Ewertz to discuss this latest twist.

It's probably just as well. If she found out she went through all that hassle unnecessarily, I'm not sure even she, with her formidable sense of humor, could handle it.

"I can see," she had said, "why people have such grim pictures on their driver's licenses."

———

Torture, 20th-Century Style

January 7, 1977

"Good afternoon. Gerble's Department Store, Miss Fleegle speaking."

"Hello. I'd like to speak to someone about an error on my bill."

"An error on your bill?"

"Yes. I keep receiving notices that I didn't pay my bill last October, but I have a canceled check to show that I did pay it and every one since."

"I'm just a switchboard operator, sir. Which department do you want to talk to?"

"I don't know. I had kinda hoped you'd know."

"Just a moment, please."

Five minutes later: "Sir? I'll connect you with bookkeeping."

"Thank you."

"Hello? Bookkeeping, Mrs. Dumpfty speaking."

"Yes. I've been receiving notices that I didn't pay my bill last October, but I have a canceled check showing that I did pay the bill."

"We don't take care of bills. You called the wrong department. Let me get the switchboard back on the line."

Three minutes later, after considerable clicking and droning, the line goes dead. The customer redials.

"Good afternoon. Gerble's Department Store. Miss Fleegle speaking."

"Hello. I just phoned a few minutes ago and was cut off or something. It was about my bill."

"Your bill?"

"Uh, I keep being billed for October, but I've . . . "

"Oh? You called a few minutes ago, didn't you? And you were cut off, huh?"

"Well, not exactly. Bookkeeping couldn't help me, and the woman there was trying to get you back on the line."

"Of course. Let me ring accounting."

"Accounting. Madge speaking. May I help you?"

"Hello. I'm trying to straighten out a billing problem. Could you help me?"

"Just a moment. I'll connect you with Mr. Harrington's office."

"Hello? Miss Duckworth speaking."

"May I speak with Mr. Harrington, please?"

"What is this regarding, please?"

210

"My charge account."

"Maybe I can help you. I'm Mr. Harrington's secretary."

"Well, your store keeps sending me notices that I didn't make my charge payment last October, but I . . . "

"I'm sorry. You'll have to speak to Mr. Harrington about that. Hold on, please."

"Harrington here. Could you hold for a second?"

"Uhhhh . . . "

Seven minutes later: "Harrington again. What can I do for you?"

"I've been receiving overdue notices from your store stating I didn't make any payment last October, but I did. Can you help me?"

"Sure. I don't handle accounts, but I can help. Let me get the switchboard girl back so she can connect you to the right department."

"No-o-o, please. I held seven minutes to . . . "

"Good afternoon, Gerble's Department Store. Miss Fleegle speaking."

"Miss Fleegle. I still haven't talked to anyone who can take care of my billing mix-up."

"Your billing mix-up?"

"I'm the one who called earlier about my October . . . "

"Didn't you phone earlier, sir?"

"Please! I don't know how much more of this I can take . . . "

"I'll connect you with accounting."

"No! You already did."

"Hmmm. Well, maybe bookkee . . . "

"How about a credit department of something?"

"Credit? Fine, sir. I'll connect you."

And: "I'm sorry, sir. That line is busy. Would you like to hold or call back later?"

211

No Music to Discuss Miss Manners by

January 18, 1984

I knew all along Miss Manners was demented.

And if she wasn't to begin with, it was only a matter of time.

Because how many times could even the strongest, most stable person write "Gentle Reader" before the mind eroded into Silly Putty?

Good ol' Miss Manners.

Judith Martin.

What do you bet she had her name changed? From Judy to Judith. And not just legally, but, to make sure it was permanent, surgically.

Miss Manners' syndicated etiquette column runs in the paper on Wednesdays.

It's not only entertaining and informative, but also makes us all better people and the world a better place to live in.

Or it used to, anyway, until this month, when MM really blew it.

Two weeks ago, MM wrote that it's rude to play soft music in a car when you have someone along or at home when you have guests who have not come over for the express purpose of music appreciation.

I couldn't believe it. I still can't.

Let me put it this way. I believe in music.

Once when I was in a good mood, I even hummed – that's how much I like music.

Maybe I don't like most country music, and maybe I

don't like opera at all, but other than that, I think music ranks right up there with the jump shot as one of humanity's crowning improvisations, disco notwithstanding.

You know the old saying: "Music hath charms to soothe the savage breast, to soften rocks or bend a knotted oak."

Of course, William Congreve did make that innocent observation nearly 300 years before the world had heard of the likes of Herman's Hermits, the Monkees, Ziggie Pop, Elton John and Rick James.

But no matter. I imagine that if he were around today, Congreve would have the most expensive stereo he could afford and would think only barbarians wouldn't enjoy hearing it in the background.

Of playing soft music in the presence of company, gentle Miss Manners wrote, "If you cannot have a pleasant conversation without a mechanical background, that is a dreadful affliction, and perhaps your guests should be warned of it. Many people, Miss Manners among them, find such conflicting noises distracting and an insult to both the conversation and the music."

Rubbish. (Look at the vile language that MM, with her outrageous opinion, has reduced me to.)

Readers? Tell me that you, too, think MM is full of starch.

And if you don't, well, then I've had it all backward for years, and who knows how many people I have *insulted*.

When we have people over, I like music playing unobtrusively. I believe music adds something, rather than gets in the way, and I've always felt we were actually *sharing* the music, not suffering from a mechanical affliction for which we should be quarantined.

And when we visit friends, I enjoy it if they play their stereos.

But is Miss Manners right? Do "many" people consider

soft music in the background a distracting insult?

Certainly, music can't really be appreciated if people are talking while it's playing. But it can be enjoyed, just the same.

So you drown out your favorite Mel Torme or Mozart tune because you were in the middle of an intellectual discourse on the designated hitter in baseball. No big deal.

What does Miss Manners do when *she* wants to share her favorite music with friends? Invite them over and insist on absolute silence? Does she allow conversation only while she's changing records? Or does she have intermissions when people can talk without feeling insulted or insulting the music itself?

Ah, but Miss Manners has taught me something I wish I'd learned long ago: that at least two people in this world (and maybe only one if MM made up the letter) do not like music to talk by. So from now on, when we have new people over, I'll ask how they feel about music before playing any.

And, as for you, Miss Manners, well, thanks for the tip. And if you're ever in our neighborhood, drop in.

For you, we will shut off the stereo, TV, blender, our son's electronic game, and, if you like, I'll even do my best to stop that distracting bathroom faucet from dripping.

———

Ban Those Babies!
Ban Those Babies!

June 22, 1988

My friend Prattlegood, who is not evil, dangerous, ferocious or even particularly grumpy as a rule, has a fascinating idea.

"I think babies should be banned," he told me.

"What?"

"Young children, too."

"*Why*, Prattlegood? Little kids aren't so bad – especially as human beings go."

"Ha! Where have you been the last million years, typo-breath? Don't you ever go out in public? Little kids are our No. 1 public nuisance now. They're worse than smokers, worse than jam boxes, worse than obnoxious drunks! Annoying little kids are everywhere anymore!"

"But you can't ban babies, Prattlegood. That might rub some people wrong."

"Well, if a ban is a little too much to hope for, I'd happily settle for some good, strong, effective baby-control laws."

"Why?"

"Why? Because the sweet little dumplings are ruining life as we know it on this planet! A person cannot go anywhere anymore without some pink-cheeked little urchin coming along and wailing and screaming."

"Come now, Prattlegood."

"Well, it's almost that bad, notebook-breath. And lately it seems like no matter where I go, little kids are there fussing, crying, throwing fits and just generally being very unnerving."

"Life is difficult, Prattlegood."

"Difficult? We are talking *torture* here, deadline-breath! I probably eat out a lot more often than most people, and it got so bad recently that if I had a sense of humor, I might have laughed at the madness of it. When I had meals in restaurants, there would be little kids squalling, and if I went into a store, there would be a little kid howling, and if I stopped at, say, a video store, there would be some sweet little half-pint all but foaming at the mouth and snarling."

"But, Prattlegood. That's the nature of little children."

"Fine. And this is my nature! To curse at their noodle-noggin'ed parents and say enough is enough already!"

"Other people don't seem to be so bothered by it, Prattlegood."

"That's only because other people are nicer than I am. But I'll bet, secretly, they'd like to break the thumbs of these kids' parents."

"So what kind of ban would you propose?"

"Baby bans – like smoking bans. There could be no-kids sections in restaurants, planes, movies, wherever."

"But maybe it's just you, Prattlegood. Maybe your nerves just aren't as good as they used to be, and that's all there is to this."

"So what? A lot of people's nerves aren't what they used to be. So we need to band together! To ban together!"

"This is pretty radical."

"Well, people like me need understanding, byline-breath. I eat out a lot. If this only happened once in a while, I might be able to handle it, even with my disposition. But when it happens every third or fourth meal, that's too often and it tells me these insensitive parents need to be taken care of."

"Maybe you just need a vacation."

"No. The problem is definitely getting worse, and in really nice restaurants, too. I mean, imagine my joy when I'm in a nice place for dinner, maybe with candlelight and soft music, and in comes two families of yahoos together with tired toddlers ready to riot."

"I feel for you, Prattlegood."

"What I propose until no-baby sections are created is that the managers of places take matters into their own hands and issue two-minute warnings to parents of squalling

216

or rowdy children. These parents are warned that if they don't stifle their little tykes in two minutes or remove them from the room, the baby bouncer, a very large, very ugly, very hairy, very menacing subhuman, will come out, get Daddy, take Daddy outside and beat Daddy to a pulp."

"That's cruel, Prattlegood."

"But the important question is, Bic-breath, is it cruel enough?"

I'm Late! I'm Late! For . . . Ah, Who Cares?

January 8, 1984

I always say I understand. I always say it doesn't bother me.

But I lie.

I don't understand, and it does bother me.

Why are people late so much?

Late for meetings, late for visits, late for dropping things off or picking things up, late for almost everything?

Doesn't being on time matter anymore?

Did it ever?

Or is it just me?

I don't get it.

If 100 people have a 3:45 flight to catch to Denver, 100 will catch it.

But if 100 people have 3:45 *invitations* somewhere, 90 of them will arrive at least 10 minutes late. Why?

I believe in being on time. But I don't take any particular pride in it. Punctuality must be the easiest of virtues.

Being on time is like tying your shoes or taking a shower.

There's nothing to it. You just do it. (Or die trying, anyway.) No big deal. Anybody can be punctual.

But I get the impression an awful lot of otherwise perfect people simply don't seem to think punctuality matters much. Maybe it doesn't.

I don't know about anybody else, but I get kind of crazy when people are much more than about five minutes late coming to our house.

I never know what to do between the time friends are expected and the time they finally arrive, because you have no idea how late they're going to be.

You don't want to turn on the TV. You might get interested in something and then have to turn it off. And who wants to go through life wondering how a "Three's Company" episode turned out?

And you certainly can't pass the time constructively by reshingling the house or painting the garage. You'd get unkempt.

But it's impossible to sit patiently reading a magazine because every two minutes your wife will hear something and call out, "Is that them?" or "They're here!" But as soon as you close the magazine, take a deep breath, retrieve a sociable mood and get all psyched up to smile and everything, your wife will look outside and say, "Oh, that's not them. It's the neighbors getting home."

"You can't wait for company like you're a timer at an athletic event," my wife explained to me once. "You can't sit there looking at your watch yelling '10 . . . 9 . . . 8 . . . 7 . . . 6 . . . 5 . . . 4 . . . 3 . . . 2 . . . 1 . . . they're late!' "

Live and learn.

But I'm even worse when it comes to getting places on time. If our family is supposed to be somewhere at 7 p.m., I pace and climb walls and prod the kids like a platoon sergeant whose troops must move out at 1845 hours at the very latest or else! *Hup! Hup! Page, where are your shoes? Chase, do you need to go to the bathroom? Where's Tracy? Anybody seen Tracy today?* That sort of thing.

"Actually," my wife said one evening recently when I was bragging about my convictions about punctuality, "I think you may be a little compulsive about being on time."

"Is that good or bad?" I gulped. "It sounds really bad. Like I can't control myself from being on time. Like I'm a lone madman terrorizing the city by going around being on time and getting annoyed when other people are late. Darn! All these years I thought I was being considerate and thoughtful, actually, I was just a sicko."

"You're not that bad," she said, trying to make me feel better.

"What I thought was my only virtue," I lamented, "turns out to be just one more character deficiency."

"Now, now," my wife said. "There are worse things than being a fanatic about being on time."

"Maybe I ought to seek counseling to learn how to control my abnormally strong feelings about punctuality," I said. "Except, come to think of it, that might be dangerous."

"Why?"

"Sicko that I am, who knows what horrible things I might do if the shrink was ever late and kept me waiting."

Cats Must
Be Morons

February 8, 1984

Some people who are no doubt in need of serious guidance will ask, "Do you like cats?"

It isn't a fair question. It is a loaded question. Keep your distance from the kind of people who look like they might ask you whether you like cats.

The only people who will indulge themselves in asking if you like cats are dangerously over-thoughtful people who either are fiercely fanatical about the joy of cats, or who attach all kinds of deep-rooted psychological significance to people's attitudes toward cats – or who do both.

Of course, the question about liking cats is really no more significant than the questions "Do you like cows?" or "Do you like squirrels?" or even "Do you like peas?"

Whether you do or don't doesn't really matter much, unless, of course, you're so obsessive about cows, squirrels or peas that you organize a new religion based on one of them, or have a pea as your best friend or something.

People who would ask you if you like cats are really deviously asking you the question in order to try you, to judge you. . . .

"Do you like cats?" screams the prosecutor.

"W-w-w-w-why, uh, sure."

"Do you have a cat?"

"No."

"When was the last time you petted a cat?"

"I don't know. I can't remember."

"Within the last year?"

"Uh, no."

"Within the last five years?"

"I doubt it."

"When you see cats, do you ever say, 'Nice kitty.' ?"

"No."

"Do you have plans to get a cat?"

"No."

Judge and jury scream together, "The defendant is guilty of not liking cats enough and is thereby guilty of all that implies. He's probably a Communist, dislikes fast food, listens to AM radio and either doesn't go to church enough or goes too much! Take him out and shoot him!"

There was a cat show at the bashed-up Broadview Hotel last weekend. I didn't find out until Monday, when it was too late.

I'm sorry I missed the cat show. It might have been my big chance to find out the real meaning of cats.

Let's face it. Cats must be morons.

About the only constructive thing they do is catch mice, and they can't even help that.

"Cat people" give cats all kinds of credit for having a lot of character and intelligence, but I can't understand why.

Cats don't show feelings. They don't sit there with their tongues hanging out, panting with irresistible charm. They don't wag their tails with happy energy. They don't tilt their heads endearingly.

They don't do anything – not after they're finished being cute, playful little kittens, anyway.

They don't do dog-like or monkey-like tricks. They don't bark at burglars and bite them. They don't tweet entertainingly like canaries. They don't lay eggs or give milk or run in the Kentucky Derby.

So what do cats do? They climb up trees and telephone poles and can't get down.

What kind of dumb animal climbs up trees and telephone poles when it can't get down?

That probably makes cats even dumber than cows.

When was the last time you had to call the fire department because your cow climbed a telephone pole and couldn't get down?

And not only are cats even dumber than cows, they probably don't taste nearly as good.

If they did, cat food would have been given a whole new meaning a long time ago by enterprising, profit-minded Americans.

No matter.

You can have cats. I prefer peas.

Arf! Arf! Arf!
Bark! Aarrroooooo!

April 24, 1988

Rude, insensitive, barking pooches are driving people bananas.

Demonic, howling hounds are causing otherwise peace-loving, God-fearing, law-abiding, decent, mannerly men and women to harbor evil thoughts of mayhem, murder and other creative forms of unpleasantness.

Behind closed doors all around the city, the state and, no doubt, the whole hairy, dog-filled world, nice, normal men and women are hunkered down pathetically in remote corners of their homes, gnawing their knuckles, clawing the walls, whimpering and praying fervently for soothing, oh-so-golden, bark-free silence. . . .

"God, if only you'll just make that doggone dog next

door stop barking so I can sleep, I'll start going to church every Easter or something! I promise!"

Yes. People are in danger of being declared clinically daffy because of barking dogs next door, two doors down, across the street or alley behind their homes, down the block.

Maybe you're one of these people, whose number, I know, is legion. After I wrote about this problem before, the response was so heavy and feverish that I've decided to try to help, good guy that I am.

So I've come up with a handy clip-out note that victims of barking dogs can give to the real culprits, the dogs' owners.

I've devised this nice, touching, plaintive clip-out plea because I've found out many people are such good or timid souls that they never even let their neighbors know the problem exists!

So read the note, check the proper spaces to tailor it to your specific problem, clip it out and then deliver it, signed or unsigned, to your neighbor by the method of your choice.

I cannot, of course, accept responsibility if this fails or backfires. I hate responsibility.

But good luck. And let me know if this does or doesn't work.

Dear Neighbor ( ), Friend ( ), Jerk ( ):

This is about your dog. Your wonderful, lovable, beautiful pet.

He ( ) She ( ) It ( ) barks ( ), howls ( ), bites ( ), eats children ( ), drools alarmingly ( ), makes a mess of my yard ( ).

Yes, nice person, your otherwise wonderful poochie ( ) beast from hell ( ) tends to bark all the time ( ), only when excited, like when tree leaves fall or a cloud drifts over ( ), early in the morning ( ), all evening ( ), all night ( ), all day ( ), while you are at work ( ), all of the above ( ), other ( ).

I don't mean to sound rude, selfish or pushy, but, well, I just don't know how much more of your nice doggy's howling I can stand before men with nets will have to come and take me away.

Your magnificent creature seems to like to bark close to the windows of the rooms in which I tend to sleep ( ), watch and try to hear TV ( ), write the Great American Novel ( ), work at home ( ), study methods of horrible medieval torture ( ), practice voodoo ( ), polish my collection of powerful, deadly weapons ( ).

I do ( ) do not ( ) wish to offend you and cause friction. But at the risk of doing so, I must tell you that your wonderful dog's barking has driven me, a generally peaceful individual who likes to mind his ( ) her ( ) own business, to consider taking you to court ( ), contacting the local bar association's Neighborhood Justice Center for mediation ( ), advertising in the paper for a hired killer ( ), breaking many of your favorite fingers and thumbs ( ), recording your mutt's howling and playing it back at high volume outside your bedroom at night ( ), sticking my head in the oven ( ), other awful stuff ( ).

I understand it isn't always easy to deal with dogs that bark a lot, but if you need assistance, may I suggest you phone a pet shop for advice? I do ( ) do not ( ) even have some ideas that might help.

If you could do something about the barking, I will be eternally grateful and might even invite you over for dinner ( ).

In closing, thank you very much for any consideration ( ), this is your last warning, ha-ha ( ), have a nice day ( )!

Sincerely, desperately and most well-meaningly yours,

(Signature optional)

So Go Have a Lousy Day!

February 17, 1984

People can be cruel. Heartless. Unfeeling.

Not often enough, maybe. But periodically.

Just ask J.P.

J.P. knows.

"I am one of the many people," J.P. begins, "who work with literally hundreds of customers every day. There are lots of us out here. We are waiters, waitresses, cashiers, tellers, receptionists, secretaries and salespeople, just to name a few.

"I've heard a complaint about us from many comedians who get laughs and applause by complaining (yet never offering a solution, I might add) because we utter the dreaded words, 'Have a nice day.'

"Whole audiences seem to hate the saying. But please, give us a break, we're only trying to be polite.

"Tell me, Mr. Getz, what else are we supposed to say? If we say nothing, we're rude. Whatever we say has to be short (who wants to hear a speech?) but friendly ('Hope you get run over by a truck' probably would not be well-received.).

"You may get tired of hearing have-a-nice-days, but try saying it 200 times a day. We need something different, something customers want to hear.

"I was hoping that you, Mr. Getz, could help us out. Perhaps you or your readers have some suggestions.

"P.S. Have a nice day, Mr. Getz!"

J.P.? You need help, serious help, but not the kind you think.

225

Your thinking is twisted. Warped.

I'm glad you wrote. You need the kind of understanding, sympathy and loving advice I have to offer in abundance.

Put briefly, J.P., you're a mess. You're too nice, too well-meaning, too thoughtful.

What's a nice person like you doing in a quandary like this?

Think about it. Here you are, a decent, agreeable, reasonable, rational, pleasant person, and you're willing to change to accommodate the boors of the world.

Forget it. If some people profess to be bothered by the pleasantry "Have a nice day," it isn't your problem, it's *theirs*.

Take my word for it. Stay nice, and don't change, no matter how many nerds you have to cuss out or punch in the lips.

J.P.? I've been around. I've seen indifference, gum-smacking waitresses and terminally preoccupied salesclerks and utterly insensitive, self-absorbed civil servants and numb, vacant-eyed receptionists and congenitally distracted, zombie-like secretaries and permanently snarling, probably rabid, cashiers.

So believe me. The world needs a lot more people who say "Have a nice day" and far, far fewer oppressively superior sophisticates who feel obligated to express intellectual outrage and sociocultural indignation over the nice, mundane pleasantries of us common people.

And don't sweat audiences who laugh at comedians' "Have a nice day" bits.

That great part-time therapist and Eagle janitor Dr. Aesop Von Getzer told me, "Hey, my guess is the people who laugh longest and loudest at have-a-nice-day jokes are the kind of decent, run-of-the-mill earthlings who, bless their phony hearts, either say 'Have a nice day' themselves

226

or go home and hide in the closet and say it."

What a shame, J.P., that "Have a nice day" is regarded by some as the lime-green, double-knit polyester leisure suit of pleasantries.

It isn't sappy or gauche. It's just the target of yet another mindless, fashionable attitude. And I can't figure how anyone can complain because some people say it when they couldn't care less what kind of day people have.

Poor *wittle* delicate souls.

Do they think that most people who say "How are you?" are genuinely interested? Or that people who say "Take it easy" care whether you actually take it easy or go get a hernia? Or that people who say "What's happening?" are dying to hear your itinerary for the day?

J.P. Stay nice and say what you please.

And if people express annoyance when you say "Have a nice day," don't apologize. Do them a favor and break their thumbs.

Severe pain will suit their dispositions much better than friendly words.

———

Thoughts I Couldn't Put a Stop to . . .

Overheard:
"Did you vote?"
"'No. I'm 70 years old. I voted enough already."

•

I think those little round wire-rimmed glasses make everybody who wears them less attractive.

Is it just my imagination or are there a lot more teenage blondes than there used to be? All of whom look exactly alike?

•

Are we going to have to hear constant, tedious references to "baby boomers" for the rest of our lives? Enough already!

•

Imagine Newsweek reporting 75 years from now, "The last baby boomer passed away Tuesday, dying with his Reeboks on . . . and still insisting he mattered."

•

I hope God turns out to be a little like Bob Newhart.

•

Not that it'll do me any good.